CATHOLIC EDUCATION

CATHOLIC EDUCATION

A Light of Truth

MONSIGNOR DENNIS MURPHY

Foreword by Joseph Sinasac

Catholic Register Books

Published in 2007 by
Catholic Register Books
1155 Yonge Street
Suite 401
Toronto, ON
M4T 1W2
www.catholicregister.org

ISBN-13: 978-0-9784389-0-6
ISBN-10: 0-9784389-0-6

Cataloguing in Publication Data available from
Library and Archives Canada

Cover design/layout: Lucy Barco
Printed and bound in Canada by Webcom Inc.

To all the Catholic educators
whose classrooms, schools
and school systems witness
to the light of the gospel

Contents

Abbreviations

Catholic Association of Religious and Family Life Educators of Ontario.......................................**CARFLEO**

Catholic Principals Council of Ontario.......................................**CPCO**

Early Childhood Education.......................................**ECE**

Education Quality and Assessment Office.......................................**EQAO**

Institute for Catholic Education.......................................**ICE**

Ontario Catholic School Trustees' Association.......................................**OCSTA**

Ontario College of Teachers.......................................**OCT**

Ontario English Catholic Teachers' Association.......................................**OECTA**

Foreword

By Joseph Sinasac

It almost seems trite to say these are momentous times for Catholic education in Ontario. Throughout the history of Canada, and particularly of this province, the times for Catholic education have always been momentous. But our own times, perhaps like all the others, have their own special uniqueness that call us to be aware and prepared to consider the responsibilities of the Catholic Church (meaning all of us) to its schools.

This book attempts to help us do just that. It is a thoughtful reading of the "signs of the times" by one of the most knowledgeable and committed actors in Catholic education of the last half century. It starts with what we fashionably call an "environmental scan," that is, a review of the cultural, political and economic environment in which the Church and its schools exist. Then, there is a diagnosis of the internal challenges facing our schools, followed by some sage advice. It is also an urgent call to action during turbulent times.

This book is a distillation of a series of essays by Msgr. Dennis Murphy which have appeared in the pages of *The Catholic Register* over the last seven years. Over this time, each of the essays has been avidly sought by school boards and various education concerns as guides for explaining the situation in which Catholic schools find themselves. Now, after repeated requests, we have decided to pull them together in one volume.

To that end, Msgr. Murphy graciously agreed to update the individual essays and write a final chapter devoted to how Catholic schools have a unique role in society to help each new generation learn to discern Truth in a world of competing claims, of venal temptations and dangerous distractions. This, as our author eloquently explains, is the prime purpose of Catholic education. It is not to teach our young people to be ready for career training (although it does that). Nor are our schools there to instil "values" or proper behaviour (though they also do that). No, Catholic schools are about much more. They are about helping our children learn the wisdom passed down by the faith of their parents – a wisdom that helps them understand they are made in the image of the one God, a God who loves them and who sends them out to love the whole world.

It is about introducing them to Jesus Christ, our Saviour and Redeemer, so that they too may share the joy of the Good News.

In this mission, one also held by the entire people of God, Catholic schools hold a special place. As Msgr. Murphy explains, the Catholic school in Ontario has the distinction (wanted or not) of being the most common meeting place today between Catholics and their Church. Catholic schools hold unique influence and unique power to pass on our faith. But they also face difficult and complex challenges – and not all from enemies beyond the gate.

As has happened so many times in Ontario history, this first decade of the new millennium faces new threats to the existence of a publicly funded Catholic school system in Ontario. We need to understand these threats – both internal and external – if we are going to face them honestly and with any hope of finding workable ways to deal with them.

Msgr. Murphy is well-positioned to help all of us to work through these challenges.

A man of multiple talents and great intelligence, he has devoted his life to the Church and its schools. A priest since 1960, Msgr. Murphy is retired now and living in North Bay, Ont., where he continues to be widely sought as a public speaker. Over the years, he has been general secretary of the

Canadian Conference of Catholic Bishops, founder and first director of the Institute for Catholic Education, a member of the Ontario Royal Commission on Learning and director of Catholic education for the Ontario Catholic School Trustees' Association.

Msgr. Murphy has given long thought to the subject of this book. It has taken shape over many talks and articles he has given over the years to teachers, principals, trustees and all those partners involved in the great project of Ontario's Catholic schools. At *The Catholic Register*, we feel especially privileged that he has turned to us to publish his thoughts and take on the task of publishing this book, the first in our new imprint, Catholic Register Books.

We hope and pray you will find this book a valuable addition to the long and fruitful discussion over Catholic education and its place in the world. In a small way, it is our contribution to the future of our children – and of our Church.

Joseph Sinasac is Publisher and Editor of The Catholic Register.

Introduction

The publicly funded Catholic school systems in Canada are rather unique institutions in the worldwide Roman Catholic Church. They are governed by and policy is made by trustees elected by fellow Roman Catholics. Almost all of these trustees are lay people. The educators from the classroom teachers to the director or superintendent of education – those who teach our children – are again almost totally lay people. These school systems and the schools within them do relate to both parish and diocese, to parish priests and the diocesan bishops in terms of pastoral and spiritual oversight. But it is hardly an exaggeration to say that in both human and economic resources the Catholic school systems are probably the largest church institutions in most dioceses – and they are governed and operated by lay people elected by the Roman Catholic population.

The school systems appear to be following a direction suggested by the Second Vatican Council almost a half a century ago. This Ecumenical Council, which has been the springboard for the development of the Church in the modern era, highlighted the role of the laity from the beginning of its deliberations. Its foundational document, *Lumen Gentium,* insisted that before all else the Church is the People of God. It was this direction that provided the new and creative approach to the role of the laity in the Church. This dogmatic constitution did not hesitate to say that "They (the laity) are in their own way made sharers in the priestly, prophetic, and kingly functions of Christ. They carry out their own part in the mission of the whole Christian people with respect to the Church and the world" (para. 31). Commenting on this document, Dom Christopher

Butler, one of the most articulate spokespersons at the time of Vatican II, saw it as a stepping stone to the future and not a final accomplishment. This same council's Decree on the Apostolate of the Laity made special mention of "teachers and educators who carry on a distinguished form of the apostolate of the laity by their vocation and office…" (para. 30).

What seems clear is that Catholic schools in Canada provide a model for new and different ways of being Church as we seek to follow where God's Spirit would have us go. These schools, like other institutions and expressions of Church life, are not perfect. In every Church institution one seeks to recognize and follow the touch of the Spirit at work in imperfect human beings. It is a form of "angelism" to expect that there will not be failings, weakness and sin in any human institution. And it is "angelism" to decry and distance oneself from institutional expressions of faith because one finds such fault and failure and sin within them.

In our country Catholic school systems are one of the few publicly funded institutions that speak deliberately and openly of transcendent values. They are recognized throughout Canada as providing first-rate education. They are also recognized as providing a learning experience that eschews a purely pragmatic and utilitarian approach dictated solely by the economic and technological needs of society. The vision and mission statements of Catholic schools bear witness to an educational approach that acknowledges the mystery, the dignity and rights of each student as a child created in the love of God and on a journey of return to this same God. In Catholic schools there is a commitment to a search for truth that we believe finds its source in Jesus Christ who revealed himself as "the way, the truth, and the life." In all of this these schools contribute much not only to the life of the Church but to public life as well.

This small book is meant to assist all with an interest in Catholic education to know something of the rich history that has brought us to this moment, to examine some of the contemporary challenges facing us, the unique role of the educator, the critical need for Christian community as the school's learning environment, the spirituality that must inspire, some suggestions regarding leadership and the search for truth in today's world.

Most of what is found in these pages was first written in a series of articles published over the last seven years in *The Catholic Register*. I would be remiss if I did not express my appreciation to the editor and publisher of this paper, Joseph Sinasac, for his constant encouragement in the writing of these articles. As well, it was at his prompting that these materials have been brought together in this book. Over the years I have often submitted manuscripts to two good and critical friends, Father Everett MacNeil and Sister Veronica O'Reilly, CSJ. I have always been grateful for the generous gift of their time and their insightful comments. As must always be said, the mistakes remain mine.

Chapter I

Confronting Religious Amnesia

The Catholic Church throughout Canada and much of the western world is being undermined by the darkness of religious amnesia. In the last number of years many of our children, their parents and the younger generation of Catholic school trustees, educators and prospective educators appear to have a fragile grounding in and sense of who we are, what our identity is and what the teaching, the stories and myths are which sustain our Catholic faith. Despite a great and wonderful goodness among many of these young people, the intentional living out of their faith is often peripheral to their daily existence. They have only a vague and unassimilated notion of the Christian and Catholic story as lived in ancient and modern times. Of many young educated Catholic adults and students it has been said that they:

> *... lack any sense of the historical perspective of Western culture in general and the part Catholicism played in the formation of that culture in particular. They ... have no sense of the kind of church which existed before the Second Vatican Council. Students have this strong conviction that what is important happens now and the "now" has little or no link with the past.* (Lawrence S. Cunningham, *The Catholic Heritage*, Crossroad, 1986)

They have not grasped the visceral imperative, "remember," so emphasized by our spiritual forebears, the Jewish people. In their hearts and minds the light of faith flickers in the prevailing winds of western secularism.

This condition is not unlike the phenomenon of so many young people today who suffer from amnesia regarding our Canadian story. Commenting some years ago on this case of national amnesia a *Globe and Mail* editorial concluded by saying, "A nation incapable of telling its own stories to successive generations will be incapable of sustaining the national conversation on which democracy depends." The Catholic community too might ask whether a religious community incapable of telling its own story to successive generations will be capable of sustaining the faith commitment on which the life of the Church depends. For a Christian, history at its deepest level reveals in the human experience the presence of the creating and saving activity of God. Through this medium of history as salvation history, God is revealed in the life of both the individual and the community. This historical perspective of Christian faith occurs amidst all of the ambiguity of determining the exact meaning and message of God acting in our human story. Not surprisingly, therefore, in examining this history one discovers that saints, sinners, rogues, heroes and schemers have always peopled the narrative. Finally, however, it is the story of ordinary folk who are a mixture of all of these. They, and the events which shape and affect them, reveal the presence, the work and the word of God.

Recent Chapters in Salvation History

To examine a few of the salient dimensions or features of Catholic education history from this perspective is in itself revealing. It suggests that in many ways the story of Catholic schools might profitably be examined as recent chapters in the history of salvation. To follow this suggestion is to read our own education history in terms of a meaning that goes beyond the political, social and economic context. It is to search our history from a faith perspective to discover a meaning that indicates to us God acting not only in our past, but in our present as well.

To begin, therefore, a few comments on some of the dimensions, the features, the people, incidents and anecdotes that created the fabric of the almost 200-year history of Catholic education in Ontario. The ultimate significance of examining this history is to be found not only in the light it casts on the past but also in what it says to the present. And that present includes problems and challenges which Catholic education faces today.

The Threat of Assimilation

The Catholic school system in Ontario and elsewhere usually originated in a small and generally impoverished group of people who found themselves in an alien environment. At risk of generalization it can be said that the Roman Catholic population of mid-19th-century Ontario was largely Irish in origin, often unlettered, considered socially inferior and lacking in clout in the halls of political power. In the new found ecumenical spirit of our times it is perhaps difficult to realize that this Catholic minority found itself surrounded by a largely Protestant and Anglican population which had little respect for them and no time for their papist religion. Their saving grace was that Ontario and Quebec were joined in a legislative union. This meant that in the Legislative Assembly their interests were often protected by the power of the French Catholic vote, which had its base in the province of Quebec.

What our Catholic forbears feared most was that they would be assimilated. Their culture, their belief system, what they held to be valuable and worthwhile, were threatened by the dominant majority in Upper Canada, now the province of Ontario. To have their own school system in which their children would not lose their identity to the generic Christianity of the public school system was the Catholic solution.

This has particular significance for our contemporary society. Roman Catholics no longer are a tiny minority. They represent approximately 35 per cent of the population, are socially integrated and are neither economically deprived nor without political clout. Catholics remain, nonetheless, a minority in an increasingly secularistic society. Many of the social and cultural institutions of our time – and one thinks here in particular of the news media – have a self-described avowedly secular agenda. This agenda often supports one public homogenized educational system as an ideal to be achieved. The media allow religion little place in the public forum – and this only grudgingly. Too often anti-religious and particularly anti-Catholic comment remains acceptable as the last refuge of bigoted and offensive commentators.

The danger now as in the mid-19th century is the danger of assimilation. Today it is the danger of losing all that is distinctive in an historical religious culture and in a belief system daily confronted with an aggressive philosophy of secularism. Despite the influence of this secular fundamentalism it can be persuasively argued that within the current political and social context the Catholic school system contributes significantly not only to the life of the Catholic Church but also to the social and cultural public life of our province and our country. It is one of the few remaining institutional presences of transcendent value in our Western world, as it seeks to create a learning environment that challenges and questions much of the value system of the dominant secularism.

The Charge of Divisiveness

In Ontario one of the earliest charges levelled against the Catholic school system from the time of its inception – and a charge which the Methodist Egerton Ryerson, the father of education in our province, at least implicitly supported – was that Catholic schools were a socially divisive force. That charge, repeated time and time again throughout the pages of history, continues to be found often enough in the letters-to-the-editor columns of many of the papers of Ontario.

As in the days of Ryerson no proof of this divisiveness has ever been demonstrated. Indeed, throughout our country and in all provinces where Catholic education is publicly funded, there is absolutely no indication that Catholic schools have caused bias, prejudice or divisiveness within their provincial communities. Moreover, although there is precious little research done in this field, the data that exist suggest quite the contrary. Longitudinal studies done in 1966 and in 1976 by the National Opinion Research Center in Chicago demonstrate that Catholic students who attend Catholic schools are much less likely to have prejudicial and racial attitudes than Catholic students who go to public schools (*The Education of Catholic Americans*, 1966, and *Catholic Schools in a Declining Church*, 1976).

Probably Catholic educators will always have to face this unsubstantiated charge. The only effective response will be by increased efforts to encourage their students through social justice and community involvement programs to make commitments to public life which reflect the unifying imperative of the gospel.

Disagreements within the Catholic Community

Then as now it could be argued that Catholic education engenders more divisiveness within the Catholic community than outside of it. Even a very cursory glance at the history of Catholic education in Ontario indicates that seldom was there universal agreement regarding various school questions. The Catholic newspapers, of which there were more than a few, involved themselves in what was often acrimonious debate regarding a variety of school questions. Their differences were often more pronounced than those now found in our contemporary Catholic press.

The educational efforts of Bishop Alexander MacDonnell, the first Catholic bishop in Upper Canada and in some ways the founder of Catholic education in Ontario, were not immune to such controversy. MacDonnell had close ties with the British authorities. Before coming to Canada, he encouraged his Scottish contemporaries to survive the difficult economic realities of the late 18th century by joining the British army. He saw no problem in maintaining loyalty to the Catholic faith and loyalty to the British government. As the first bishop of the new diocese of Kingston, Ontario (1826), he found that ecclesiastical honours were soon followed by political recognition. MacDonnell was appointed a member of the Legislative Council and took his seat in 1831. He was a confidante of Sir John Colbourne, the Lieutenant Governor of Canada, and of Lord Bathhurst, the Colonial Secretary in London. In all of this he was not short of adversaries, including priests, within the Catholic community. It is not difficult to believe that the Irish community of Ontario considered his relationship with the British authorities as supping with the devil. They would at best be suspicious of one perceived as taking the British coin in support of Catholic schools. What is clear in all of this is that from the beginning disagreement was an everyday reality within the Catholic school community.

Long before their role was more clearly delineated by the Second Vatican Council (1962-1965), the laity emerged as powerful actors in this drama, particularly in the kind of lay control gradually exercised by predominantly lay trustees and educators. These lay Catholic leaders in many instances did not hesitate to challenge the leadership of the clergy. From 1882 to 1903 James Frances White was an inspector of separate schools, a predecessor of current supervisory officers. Not only did he oppose the Ontario bishops regarding teacher certification but he went on to win the day in this struggle. In the 1930s the trustee Martin Quinn was a founder of the Catholic Taxpayers Association and in this capacity he responded to Archbishop Neil McNeil's question as to why the Catholic laity did not seem to interest themselves in schools questions: "They fear that in the final analysis, their work is quite likely to be destroyed by faulty judgment on the part of the hierarchy, followed by ill-considered action on their part."

Assessed through such historical lenses the phenomenon of disagreement in Ontario's Catholic education community tends to relativize our present disputes.

The Religious

One cannot recount any history of Catholic education in the province without highlighting the role of the religious communities of men and women. If the ecclesiastical leaders, and many of the high-profile lay leaders, were the architects and engineers of Catholic education in Ontario, it was the teachers and principals of the schools in the early days who were the bricklayers and stonemasons. Theirs was the task of drawing the stones and placing them laboriously one upon the other in order to provide the quality education system in which the Catholic community in Ontario takes justifiable pride today. Most prominent among these teachers and principals were the religious, and particularly religious women.

Not for them the hurly-burly of political intrigue, editorial comment, or thundering denunciation. Rather, from the beginning, they provided the human resources which assured that, with meagre funds, a school system would develop that respected at once the practical educational needs of mainly immigrant people and the educational heritage of Catholic education. The story has yet to be told adequately of the sacrifices which they made, sleeping in attics above schools and living on the sparest of rations.

Their contribution raises the question whether a significant and distinctive Catholic education system will ever exist unless some group of people is sufficiently committed with that passionate belief that inspires extraordinary and heroic sacrifices.

Significant Reforms – a Poisoned Chalice?

Throughout the history of Catholic education in Ontario many of the various educational reforms were replete with all of the ambiguity that usually attends any significant institutional change. One example is the eagerness with which the Catholic education community accepted the establishment of the larger units of administration in 1969. This was a significant moment. The establishment of the larger units had been legislated for the public school system. It was then requested by the Catholic education community. The motivation of Catholic educators at that time was surely to provide a better quality of education for some of the small and less affluent Catholic boards. With this change, however, there was a lessening of parental influence on school boards and in the running of individual schools. To some extent the home-school-parish relationship was negatively affected by this change.

Similar comments could be made about the Foundation Tax Plan in the early 1960s. As more money flowed to Catholic schools because of this legislation, an attendant increase in government control followed.

The eagerness of Catholic educators to accept the legislative enactments of Bill 30 in 1985-86 (providing full public funding to the end of high school) also carried a price. These included the open access provisions to Catholic secondary schools and the temporary loss of discriminatory hiring rights which threaten that essential component of Catholic education which is the creation of a Catholic community in our schools.

Of more recent vintage, in the late 1990s, is the very explosive and divisive conflict that arose within the Catholic community over Bill 160, particularly as this bill affected the right of Catholic schools boards to set tax rates.

The goal of Catholic educators for years had always been equitable funding – the guarantee that the Catholic system could provide education along with the public system on a level playing field. What was clear from the beginning was that the cost of equity would be further government control over both systems. For Catholic educators the unrecognized cost at the time was the long and ugly battle between the Ontario Catholic School Trustees' Association (OCSTA) and the Ontario English Catholic Teachers' Association (OECTA).

Probably we remain too close to the events that transpired to provide cool and rational evaluation of them. As with most historical events, proximity to them often clouds rather than clarifies their ultimate significance.

There remain, nonetheless, significant questions which continue to be much discussed today. For example, in their quest for equitable funding, did the OCSTA in supporting the funding provisions of Bill 160 surrender too much? Did they lose too much of the important practical control that comes with taxing power? And in opposing Bill 160 was the OECTA principally motivated in its struggle against the bill's taxing provisions by a desire to maintain the "Catholicity" of the system as they claim? Could/should the bishops have intervened more forcefully, at least at the level of ascertaining where the truth of the matter lay in the early moments of this discussion? Should the Ontario Catholic Supervisory Officers' Association have remained on the sidelines as this battle escalated? Would any of the Catholic parties have entered this fray if they had known how acrimonious it would become and what the ultimate cost would be? And what is the final result in terms of funding for our Catholic schools? All of these are questions which we must continue to examine. The way we answer them will surely be affected by the unanimous decision of the Supreme Court of Canada, which determined that the province of Ontario in its new funding legislation did not offend the constitutional rights of Catholic schools. No doubt definitive answers to all these questions will continue to elude us for some time.

In all of these instances – from the Scott Act in 1863 to Bill 160 – the question must be asked whether we drank a "poisoned chalice." What price did Catholic education pay for large units of administration, for the Foundation Plan, for Bill 30 and the completion of the Catholic education system, and for equity in funding? Some claim that the price was too high. Others counter by saying that many of the strategic concessions gradually achieved the possibility of Catholic education for students both rich and poor, and from every stratum of Ontario's Catholic community. In addition, they say, the Catholic system reflects for the first time all levels, convictions, strengths and weaknesses of the broader Catholic community.

In all of these events, and in the *dramatis personae* who played them out on the stage of history, the question remains how one recognizes in this story of ours the hand and the word of God. What do these recent chapters of salvation history mean for us? The closer these events are to the present the more difficult the discernment becomes. But that discernment remains always the task of the Catholic community. We are called finally to discern the word of God not only in the past, but in the present educational realities with which we are faced.

Government Policies and Their Consequences

No Ontarian who has been paying the slightest attention in recent years doubts that the context for education has altered radically in the province. Some attempted to reduce these reforms to nothing more than part of the neo-conservative agenda of the Harris government of the late nineties.

However, similar educational reforms also took place in many jurisdictions in the Western world. The recommendations of the Royal Commission on Learning (1995), in its report *For the Love of Learning*, did not share the political ideology of the aforementioned Conservative government. Yet this report called for significant educational changes, many of which were taken up by that government, even if the manner and purpose of their reforms appeared to be quite contrary to the spirit of the Royal Commission report.

From this period on there was a new context for education in Ontario. It has had very important, not to say radical, consequences for the Catholic education system. What follows is a brief description of six elements of this new context and some of the consequences these have for the Catholic education system.

Curriculum

A new curriculum based on clearly defined expectations at the various grade levels was mandated and is still being created through the Ministry of Education. This curriculum is characterized by a more rigourous content. In many cases it has advanced the teaching of certain concepts to an earlier grade.

A fortunate consequence for Catholic education has been the development of distinctive curriculum materials for Catholic schools. These materials attempt to bring to all of the different subjects or disciplines the distinctive approach to education which is the hallmark of Catholic education. Such a curriculum insists, therefore, not only on knowledge and skills — as does the curriculum for the public system — but also on certain value expectations.

What is necessary for this curriculum to be successful and reflective of the peculiarity of Catholic education is that teachers at both the pre-service and in-service levels be familiar with it and prepared to use it. To some extent this has been attempted. At the in-service level summer institutes were funded by the government and staffed by the teacher federations. However, for student teachers intending to teach in the Catholic school system, the faculties of education still in most cases have no programs to prepare teachers for these distinctive curriculum materials. Nor are many teachers, particularly in Catholic secondary schools, sufficiently aware of the Catholic education implications in their particular subjects or disciplines.

Accountability

In our current atmosphere of accountability it is not surprising that transparent accountability is demanded at every level of the education system. People want to know, "Who does what?" Over the last several years new levels of accountability have been demanded of trustees, teachers, principals, supervisory officers, directors of education and all those involved in the educational enterprise. What remains less clear is the extent to which this accountability applies to the faculties of education, as indicated above, and to the Ministry of Education itself.

For Catholic schools, such insistence on accountability requires at the board level distinctive indicators for our distinctive system. Trustees must assure the distinctiveness of Catholic belief and practice not only in board policy on school and curriculum matters but in policy on administration matters or labour relations, on contracting out, and on the way all business is done. As well, the practical and personal expectations outlined in the OCSTA document *Witnesses to Faith* should be uniformly applicable to all trustees and educators.

Centralization

Increasing centralization in the areas of funding, curriculum development and policy making have been part of educational reform in the last few years. This has had particular curriculum implications sounding warning bells in the Catholic education community from the beginning. Although, as mentioned above, a distinctive curriculum for Catholic schools continues to be developed and funded by the government, concern remains that the centralizing of this dimension of education can create a tension between a government's political ideologies on the one hand, and Catholic school systems on the other. A particularly striking example of this tension arises when the social justice dimension of Catholic education, which should permeate all subjects, stands at an oblique remove from government policy especially in areas such as life issues and social welfare.

The centralized and equitable funding of education also raises two serious questions that Catholic educators must face.

In the first place, because funding now follows the student, Catholic school boards in their secondary schools must resist the temptation to attract as many students as possible regardless of their faith in order to increase the available funding. The effects of such attitudes will effectively undermine efforts to create Christian community which must be the fundamental learning environment of a Catholic school.

Secondly, the following question must be faced: With the same funding available to every student in the province, how does the Catholic school system fund those extra dimensions of education which are part and parcel of its educational package? This question will be treated in greater detail below.

New Roles

School trustees, principals and supervisory officers are often called to play roles quite different from those of the past. The principal responsibility of the trustee – albeit not a new one – is to be a policy maker. Principals have become not only curriculum leaders and administrators but also the chief catalysts in the process of bringing the community into the educational process. This latter responsibility they share with supervisory officers and directors of education. The "community" for a Catholic school will embrace not only various civic institutions and businesses but, in keeping with Catholic school tradition, the local church community as well.

Obvious consequences follow as to how Catholic boards legislate and how educators implement policies. Of special importance is a new kind of partnering with "the Church." This is unique to Catholic schools and will accompany their partnering with various industrial and commercial enterprises.

New Institutions

In less than a decade Ontario's education scene witnessed

the establishment of several new and significant institutions. Chief among them are the Ontario College of Teachers (OCT) and the Education Quality and Assessment Office (EQAO). The former is now responsible for the many different aspects of teaching as a profession. The latter is charged with assessing and evaluating all levels of the province's educational system. There is, as well, an increased interest by parents, educators and government in early childhood education (ECE). This interest, unfortunately, has yet to be translated into serious government support for this "new kid on the block."

The College of Teachers appears to increasingly recognize the uniqueness of the Catholic school system and of the particular pre-service and in-service programs it requires. It is probably the OCT, through its accreditation process for faculties of education, which will determine how the unique needs of student teachers headed for the Catholic school system are to be met by the faculties.

At the level of the EQAO, however, there seems to be little current recognition of the fact that the expectations of Catholic schools are different from those of the public schools and require particular forms of assessment and evaluation.

In the area of early childhood education, educators are increasingly aware that ECE is of particular benefit to the most marginalized and vulnerable children in our society. Should it not, therefore, be of particular importance to Catholic educators and given priority in requests to government concerning changes in the current funding formula?

Assessment, Evaluation and Reporting

Ontario's Ministry of Education has moved to assure the use of standardized processes of evaluating and assessing students. Standardized report cards are part of its overall strategy. Serious questions remain as to how the data and information learned can best help student learning. The whole matter of assessing, evaluating and reporting in the disciplines of religious and family life education has not yet been resolved within the Catholic education community and the Ministry of

Education. There still remains considerable debate as to whether the provincial report card is adequate in the area of religious education at the elementary level and how it is that such reporting should take place at the secondary level.

Finding Our Way into the Future

Never before has there been a greater need for a clearly articulated, strategic plan for the Catholic school system and for the Catholic Church in our province. Such a plan must take into consideration the current realities of our Church, and of its largest and most significant institutional expression, the Catholic school system. Discrete pastoral strategies for parish, school and diocese are not adequate. An integrated pastoral approach at both the provincial and local board and diocesan levels is necessary.

Such a strategic plan will require the input, the co-operation and the resources of all of the partners in Catholic education and in our Church. One need be neither a Cassandra nor a Jeremiah to recognize that the educational and political directions of the current moment severely challenge the existence of Catholic education as a publicly supported system. Catholic education in Ontario has never been more seriously threatened – and this at a time when many of the various players have not had their act together. The moment is long past when busily blaming one another for the current situation will be of service to anyone or any group.

A Few Harsh Realities

Outside of the Catholic education community there appears to be only precarious and declining support for the Catholic school system as it now exists in Ontario. To deal with this situation the first thing required is a serious reality check about our Catholic school system and our Catholic Church.

To speak of the latter for a moment is to recognize that whatever figures one cares to use, most of the Roman Catholics in the province of Ontario do not participate on any regular basis in the life of the Church. What is evident everywhere is a high level of disenchantment with the Church by both young and middle-aged Catholics. These latter attach no great credibility to the teaching of the Church, particularly on moral issues. Hardly anyone pays attention to Church teaching on birth control, and this arguably is the reason for a lack of credibility in other areas, particularly areas of personal morality.

Catholic young people are quite convinced that premarital sexual relationships do not pose a moral question but one of health and social convenience. Younger Catholics particularly have been profoundly affected by the individualism and relativism of contemporary western society. The self has become the arbiter of personal moral choice. Each one decides what is right or wrong, and no one person, tradition or institution is allowed to advise otherwise (cf. John Fulton et al., *Young Catholics at the New Millennium,* University College Dublin Press, 2000).

Catholics generally believe that people who have been divorced and remarried should with sufficient cause be allowed to participate fully in the Eucharist. Celibacy as an absolute requirement for the priesthood is considered unnecessary by most Catholics and an ideal which only a few of those called to the priesthood can or should attain. Few deny the need for serious changes in the role of women in the Church. Commitments and fidelity in what has been called our "three minute culture" are temporary at best. In our highly individualistic culture the social teaching of the Church finds little resonance among people who prefer tax cuts to better social welfare programs. As all this happens, those who have traditionally provided the leadership in our community, priests and religious, are fewer and fewer in number and greyer and greyer in appearance.

As mentioned earlier, another reality that must be faced is that our young people do not know the story of our faith. Those professors who teach the religious education courses in the faculties of education are unanimous in reporting that very many of the Catholic students — those who intend to teach within our Catholic school system — are, in large part, religious illiterates as far as the Catholic and Christian story is concerned.

Many of the young people in our Catholic secondary schools betray an obvious lack of familiarity with the Eucharist, how to participate in it and how to comport themselves. They betray both a lack of any sense of the sacred and of any conceptual context within which to place the Eucharist as the centre of our Catholic life. Such fundamental questions as the nature and meaning of sacraments and how sacraments have been traditionally understood in the life of the church are understood in very incomplete fashion by students in many of our elementary schools. This religious illiteracy may be due in part to the failure in the schools, but mainly it is the result of children from families in which faith is given little practical.

To summarize: Most of the Catholics in the province of Ontario do not practise their faith. Not surprisingly, their children who go to Catholic schools do not know the story of faith, or the attitudes to faith that come from family and which are its sustaining foundation. The student teachers in our faculties of education, and I would suggest many of our younger teachers, although wonderfully eager and talented young people, are quite blissfully unaware of our story. Priests and religious, who traditionally would be called on to respond to this situation are too old and too few to deal with this challenge. We are in the process of forgetting who we are.

What to Do?

It is painful to paint the Catholic education landscape in colours as bleak as this. However, to do otherwise would be less than honest. There does remain hope if we will grasp the nettle. A few suggestions, therefore, regarding our way into the future. Ultimately, we need a province-wide strategic pastoral plan for both our Church and the Catholic school system in the province. Such a plan must recognize that we have many more pupils in our schools than we have worshippers in our churches. What follows is not such a plan but suggestions regarding certain elements which it must include.

A New Language in a Community of Faith

At the present moment in the life and development of the

Catholic Church we find ourselves in the uncertainty of "between times." This is particularly evident in the realization that our language, our words, our teaching, do not seem to have the power to communicate that they once possessed. More is involved here than children not knowing our story, tradition and heritage, of suffering from religious amnesia.

We are also in urgent need of new words, of a new language to tell our story – a language which resonates with contemporary experience and which can communicate with the present generations. The language will have the power to change lives, to transform our students, however, only if it is heard in a community of faith. Each of these challenges will be developed more completely in the chapter which follows.

Evangelizing before Catechizing

From the forgoing one could conclude that the first insistence must be on assuring that our story and its teachings, beliefs and moral codes be told in clear and uncompromising fashion in all of our schools – and told in a new language. This surely is necessary. But of equal necessity is facing the fact that kids who come from non-practising families live in a formative context of practical atheism. There is a huge question as to whether or not one can call them believers as they enter a Catholic school classroom. If they are not believers then we should speak not of catechesis but of conversion; and conversion follows upon both pre-evangelizing and the preaching or announcement of the gospel. This has consequences for how we teach in Catholic schools. A few of these consequences follow.

i) William J. O'Malley, a Jesuit who has taught for many years in a Catholic high school in the Bronx, insists that only if we are ruthlessly honest about where the kids in our classrooms are these days will we be able to get to them (*America*, Sept. 16, 2000). He claims that teachers in Catholic schools today almost have to be apologists. They have to prepare the ground before ever announcing the Christian message. O'Malley says that the only sane place to begin with students is through creating a felt need in them for some consistent worldview, something that will make sense out of death and the moral ambiguities that every human being faces. To do this we must tell young people above all else that they are worthwhile. Young people want to hear that message even though they may not realize how much they want to hear it.

A Catholic school should at least provide then a precious zone of personal stability in which a young person can grapple with these kinds of questions aided and abetted by the educators. Students need a place where there is some coherence. If we create this coherent and consistent zone of stability then according to O'Malley we can put forward four non-negotiables of Christian faith:

Jesus is the embodiment of God. Somehow God came from behind time and space to show us how it is done.

Jesus/God died in order to rise and show us that we are immortal and to share divine aliveness with us.

Those who belong to Jesus/God see the values of "The Kingdom" (them first – God and neighbour) as more important then the values of "The World" (me first).

We celebrate that incorporation in a serving community and a weekly meal of thanksgiving.

ii) In our elementary schools we should put emphasis on teaching children to pray. Never before has prayer been so essential to maintain individual faith as in our increasingly secular society. Perhaps centring prayer or some prayer which uses the imagination would best be taught to them before their religious imagination is in some way atrophied by secularism.

iii) Catholic schools today need an EQAO approach to determine both the level of religious literacy and how to provide whatever remedial help is necessary. Surely by now those who argue that religious faith is not measurable have come to realize that there are religious skills and knowledge which are measurable and assessable. Not to assess kids in this way is to suggest that it is unimportant to know the richness of our Catholic tradition, heritage and culture, and be able to articulate it.

Teacher Assistance and Preparation

If there is to be some integrated pastoral, educational strategic plan then at the centre of it must be the way in which we commit to support the needs of the teachers within our system.

Our Catholic education community has argued effectively and successfully in the courts of the land that the teacher is at the heart of the Catholic educational enterprise. These arguments were sufficient to convince a judge of the Ontario Supreme Court that section 136 of the Education Act should be expunged. With the passing of the legislation to complete the Catholic school system in 1985-1986 there was – at the insistence of the New Democratic Party – a clause (136la) inserted which legislated that after a 10-year period Catholic schools would no longer have the right to discriminate in hiring practices. This effectively meant that Catholic boards could no longer control the entrance into the Catholic schools of people who did not share the distinctive educational philosophy and goals of the Catholic school system. The indisputably secular Ontario courts, however, struck down this legislation as injurious to the Catholic school system and in violation of our constitutional guarantees. Mr. Justice Sharpe, in rendering his judgment, argued persuasively about the centrality of Catholic teachers as witnessing to and handing on the faith, culture and tradition which are essential to the Catholic education community.

The question posed today is this: If the Catholic teacher is at the heart of the Catholic educational process and essential to it, how will the Catholic school system ensure that its teachers are well able to transmit its story, create its culture in the community of the school and speak in all disciplines the language of Catholic faith? From the earlier discussion it is clear that many students in faculties of education, and many young teachers currently engaged in Catholic schools, are unfortunately unable to do this.

There have been some remarkably successful efforts at seeking to address this question over the last number of years. One thinks of the three-part course in religious education sponsored by the OECTA and the OCSTA. Over the past 25 years there have been, as well, intensive efforts to persuade faculties of education to offer courses which would adequately prepare those teachers who intend to teach in Catholic schools for the kind of education that is particular to these schools. Not much success has been met in this latter endeavour, however, even following the clear recommendation of the report of the Royal Commission in Learning in 1995.

The Catholic education community definitely requires major initiatives at this time over and above the three-part OECTA/OCSTA religious education courses, the course offered by the Catholic education community to prospective supervisory officers (Supervisory Officers Qualification Program), the laudable efforts in professional development of both OECTA and the Catholic Principals Council of Ontario (CPCO), the Catholic leadership programs at several universities, and the current religious education courses offered in the faculties of education.

Leading Catholic educators in the province acknowledge that what is of primary importance for teachers is to know something of the history of Catholic education in the province, to be exposed to the philosophical underpinnings of Catholic education, to have a clearer sense of the story, tradition, heritage and culture of Catholicism, and to understand how all of this affects both the development and implementation of curriculum. In short, some kind of in-service which will be supported by all of the Catholic education associations in the province is required, whatever the cost of that may be.

As far as pre-service programs in the faculties of education are concerned, there is now needed the uncompromising political will to pursue the introduction of such courses, just as the Catholic education community has pursued other major objectives in its 180-year history. The Ontario College of Teachers has come to recognize that there is an individual and unique philosophy of education with considerable curriculum consequences in the Catholic school system. This acknowledgement of the need for distinctive courses has in large measure followed upon the development of publicly funded curriculum materials peculiar to the Catholic system. The OCT seems willing to press the faculties of education to respond to this acknowledged need.

The Catholic education community does not have the luxury, however, of continuing to draw this process out with the glacial speed which seems to have accompanied it in the past. It is a matter of such urgency that it requires the Catholic education community to act now lest those responsible for handing on the language, the story and the culture of our faith fail in their task because they themselves are not sufficiently familiar with this heritage and tradition.

Early Childhood Education

An integral part of distinctive Catholic education should be a commitment to early childhood education whether or not the government moves in significant fashion to fund this important dimension of education. ECE has been shown to significantly advance and assist in the education of all children – most recently by the two reports on the subject authored by Dr. Fraser Mustard and Norrie McCain in 1999 and 2007. As already mentioned, however, the value of ECE becomes particularly clear in the case of the most vulnerable and marginalized of students. Given this fact, Roman Catholic schools should have a particular commitment to these socially disadvantaged students. In keeping with the "option for the poor," which is central to the gospel message, Catholic schools should be in the vanguard of any educational direction and programming which addresses the needs of children on the edge of the educational process. Even if the government fails to move in this direction in the near future, Catholic schools should take leadership in this important educational development.

A Catholic Institute Adequately Funded

Both in the United States and in England considerable discussion and momentum has developed concerning the establishment of academic research and development facilities of teaching and learning within the Catholic education tradition.

If Catholic education in Ontario is to continue to grow and to develop, as it must, it would seem that nothing less is required in Ontario. Our efforts, for example, in the areas of teacher preparation and development and of Christian models of early childhood education will require such a facility.

Whether this be through the establishment of a new institution or by properly funding the research objectives of the present Institute for Catholic Education (ICE) is unimportant. What is important is that this matter be addressed forthwith as a major component of a provincial Catholic education strategy for finding our way in this new millennium.

Funding Catholic Education

All of the above will require more funding than is currently spent. What is becoming ever more obvious is that the critical dimension of Catholic education not found in secular education does involve an added expense. With the advent of equitable funding, Catholic students now receive funding on a par with their counterparts in the public system. However, Catholic schools offer extra programs in areas such as religious education, family life education, pastoral care departments and the like. Arguably, ECE programs and community education initiatives should also be given priority. These "extras" in Catholic schools require extra curriculum materials, resource people, space and facilities, professional development and so on. And importantly, there is the present and urgent need to remedy the religious amnesia described above. The Catholic school system is badly in need of funding for these urgent necessities.

If it is true that more Catholics touch the life of the Church at the level of the school than elsewhere, there is a certain logic in suggesting that the whole Church should come to the aid of the school at this particular historical moment. The monies needed to fund the "extra" dimensions of Catholic education should not be obtained by asking educators and other school board employees to accept lower salaries. The monies necessary to respond to the kind of crisis which has been described herein should come from the broad Catholic community. We live now a challenge which involves all Roman Catholics and all should be asked to respond to this pressing need.

Earlier mention was made of the considerable sacrifice which religious, especially women religious, made to ensure the survival and development of Catholic education. Without these religious communities we would not have Catholic education today.

The time for sacrifice has not passed. At this moment, should it not be, or could it not be, parishes and dioceses which come to the aid of the school system, at least in providing that "extra" so critically needed at the present moment? Could not dioceses and parishes institute regular funding appeals that would ensure the immediate introduction of the proper programs for aspiring Catholic teachers, even before such are introduced into the faculties of education? Could these same institutions not guarantee the financial support for the necessary in-service programs, professional development in religious and family life education, the provision of pastoral care – and all of the necessary extras that make up Catholic education? Funding is needed now for community education and ECE programs that reflect Catholic thinking, and for research and development facilities which will articulate this thinking. It would seem clear that such sacrifice would have its own benefit within parishes and dioceses as well.

This has not been the usual practice in Ontario in recent years. However, certainly in an earlier era and in different countries, in different times and places, dioceses and parishes have come to the aid of the Catholic school system. What is being suggested here is that we are living one of those moments in Ontario where events challenge us to respond to a moment of crisis. If there is no will to move in this direction it is difficult to foresee a long future for Catholic schools in Ontario. The Catholic community is being called to write another chapter in its history, in the history of salvation.

Chapter II

The Challenges from Within

As outlined in the previous chapter, over the better part of two centuries hundreds, indeed thousands, of committed people have been convinced that their Catholic schools were a treasure of great worth. Lay people, especially parents; clergy, both priests and bishops; religious women and men; trustees and teachers – all recognized the unique and distinctive value of Catholic schools. And they recognized that these schools would continue to exist only if together they sacrificed and struggled against all of the pressures and forces which directly or indirectly sought to abolish them. It was relatively easy in most times to recognize those forces hostile to the Catholic school system.

In recent years, however, an increasing number of people are suggesting that the threat to the Catholic school system is not so easily recognizable. It no longer comes from outside. The threat, they say, is from within. In the words of Pogo, the cartoon character created by Walt Kelly, "We have seen the enemy and it is us." One may choose to agree or disagree with this assessment. Certainly opposition external to the Catholic school system continues to exist. However, from within what seems particularly disturbing is the lack of common effort, commitment and consensus about what fundamental goals and objectives should be occupying our attention and energies at the present time.

It can hardly be debated that in the present moment all social institutions and programs are increasingly scrutinized as to their relevance. Bernard Blishen in his study of Ontario's Catholic schools done for the Institute for Catholic Education and published in 1990 warned: "In the present era of rapid social change, one of the most important conditions for institutional continuity is consensus among members about basic institutional values and objectives." And he went on to say, "Since its founding the Church has survived because it has been able to maintain this basic consensus on its objectives. This is particularly evident in the Ontario Catholic school system's struggle for full social and legal legitimacy" (p. 36).

Few would argue that with the completion of the Catholic system to the end of secondary school in 1985-86, and with the advent of equitable funding in the next decade the quest for social and legal legitimacy has in large part been realized. The questions that face us now, however, are whether there are new challenges which confront us, what they are and whether there exists within the Catholic school community the necessary consensus to deal with them.

An Environmental Scan of Our Church and Society

Both organizations and individuals speak today of the need to do what is called an environmental scan when considering such questions. Such a scan examines personal and communal experiences, the world around us, the tasks we perform, the relationships that make up our lives, and the often contradictory drives and passions that give us direction. An environmental scan can help to identify at least some of the dominant factors currently shaping and affecting our lives in our society, our schools, and our Church.

For Christians this represents something more than a sociological exercise. For us, identifying and naming our personal and communal experiences is also a way to recognize the words and the language through which God reveals his face to us. The great Spanish mystic John of the Cross tells us that "the language of God is the experience God writes into our lives."

An environmental scan for Catholic educators searching out the meaning of the present moment and some guidance for their way into the future must include at least a summary consideration of the present situation of both society and Church, including a decreasing level of practice and credibility, a lack of transparency in the Church, the aggressive and often hostile secularism of the times, the religious illiteracy of our younger generations, and the contemporary expressions of our never ending search for God. A word about each.

Faltering Practice and Credibility in the Church

Well before the scandals which have recently rocked our Catholic community there was an evident disenchantment with the Church by many Catholics both young and middle-aged. Participation in the life of the Church is peripheral to the daily experience of most Roman Catholics in the province of Ontario – and in most of the western world. As already mentioned even those Catholics who do participate in the life of the Church attach decreasing credibility to its teaching, particularly on moral issues. In issues of personal morality, especially in the area of human sexuality, in the ever increasing number of bioethical questions arising from new forms of human conception, in the matter of clerical celibacy, the ordination of women, in the demands of Church teaching on social justice, Catholics, especially younger Catholics, have in large part moved towards the moral relativism of much of contemporary western society.

This situation is not helped by the fact that those who have traditionally provided the leadership in our community, priests and religious, are fewer in number and greyer in appearance. Nor is it helped by the reality of parents who fail to encourage their sons and daughters to follow the call to the priesthood or religious life.

A Lack of Transparency

In recent years as Catholics have sought to cope with the humbling reality of sexual abuse by the clergy, what has surfaced beyond this shame is the discovery within our Church of a climate of secrecy and a lack of transparency. It is a secrecy and lack of transparency not only in dealing with sexual abuse by the clergy. This latter tragedy has served to reveal a similar hiddenness surrounding decision-making especially regarding the appointments of both priest and bishops. This hiddenness allows little clarity as to the reasons that prompt various pastoral appointments. How the members of the Church, of a diocese or parish benefit remains obscure. Such practices run the threat of sustaining a clerical culture which too easily can be tempted to place clerical concerns and ecclesiastical politics above the pastoral care of God's people. Not unrelated is that the promise of lay participation, especially through parish and diocesan pastoral councils as encouraged by Vatican II, seems to have fallen on hard times.

Aggressive Secularism

As all of this has transpired within the Church, a supposedly neutral secularism has shown a face often openly hostile to all religious belief. This almost fundamentalist secularism supports an increasingly value laden agenda that would deny believers a voice in the public discussion regarding the policies and directions of government. The Catholic Church – and in many cases the Christian Church – is in disfavour not only because of clergy sexual abuse. It is also in disfavour because its social teaching criticizes a society that continues to elect at both the provincial and federal levels governments whose priorities are to make the rich richer rather than address issues like child poverty and shameful global disparities of wealth. Catholics and other religious groups are in disfavour because of opposition to government policies that reduce social assistance to single parents, marginalize the poor and weak and make economic growth the ultimate goal of society. Catholics are in disfavour today because of continued attention to these and other life issues such as abortion and euthanasia. Catholics are in disfavour for refusing to accept that premarital and extramarital sex is behaviour that is value-neutral – behaviour that has no consequences on human sexuality and the family. The avowedly secular agenda of many of the social and cultural institutions of our time – particularly the news media – is often diametrically opposed to these Church positions.

This same secularistic agenda also supports more often

than not one public homogenized educational system as an ideal to be achieved. Like the forces perennially urging separatism in Quebec, in Ontario there are those individuals and organizations who with great regularity campaign for the abolition of the Catholic school system. Usually this opposition to Catholic schools is based on a U.S. model of separation of church and state – a model antithetical to our Canadian history of church-state relationships. The matter is compounded by much of the media, which often reject out of hand any place for religion in discussions about contemporary public issues. Unfortunately anti-religious and particularly anti-Catholic comment remains one of the last politically correct and acceptable forms of social commentary.

The Search for God

The paradox is that amidst the humbling of the church, the aggressiveness of the secularists, faltering Catholic practice and credibility there remains as a dominant feature of our times a pervasive search for God. And it is a search that suggests a sense of urgency. The Canadian sociologist Reginald Bibby's ongoing surveys seem to indicate that there is an increase again in participation in Church life in Canada. We can take some consolation in that. But of greater significance are surely other signs of the times.

In 1991 best-selling Canadian author Douglas Coupland published his book, *Generation X*. It examined the lives of his contemporaries – lives he described as empty of meaning, hopeless lives lived in a culture of conspicuous consumerism, and saturated with media. A few short years later (1994) he published *Life after God*. This series of short stories told again the disillusionment of his contemporaries. In the last story in the latter book after describing the after-twenties lives of his friends, the main character concludes his story with these words: "Now – here is my secret: I tell it to you with an openness of heart that I doubt I shall ever achieve again, so I pray that you are in a quiet room as you hear these words. My secret is that I need God – that I am sick and can no longer make it alone. I need God to help me give, because I no longer seem to be capable of giving; to help me be kind, as I no longer seem capable of kindness; to help me love, as I seem beyond being able to love" (p. 359).

In the popular poet and songwriter Leonard Cohen's CD, *Ten New Songs,* he talks about "Boogie Street." This is Cohen's synonym for life. He writes and sings this: "Tho' all the maps of blood and flesh / Are posted on the door / There's no one who has told us yet / What Boogie Street is for."

Our society no less than people of every age want to know, have to know, what Boogie Street is for. In our bookstores these days one finds ever so many titles trying to tell us what Boogie Street, what life is for. Everything from New Age mysticism to the *Celestine Prophecies* is about the search for a meaning beyond ourselves and our material possessions.

Unfortunately, perhaps, the vast majority of these spiritual self-help tomes seek to lead the individual to find meaning in life only within the self. However, there is another phenomenon of our times – a phenomenon which recognizes that a self-centred search for meaning in life surrenders only a very partial understanding of the human journey. More and more people today are searching to discover some coherent and consistent sense of meaning and direction within their families, their ancestors, their history, their story. It is sometimes called the "roots" phenomenon.

Probably this latter phenomenon comes about because we are experiencing ourselves as a people without any real continuity in our lives, a people whose story has been so deconstructed and relativized that we appear to be nothing of significance, to be hardly worthwhile. Almost intuitively we sense that it is our story, or our history, which gives some sense of direction, some meaning and some importance to our personal lives. Without a story, a history, we sense that the human journey has no meaning because it has no coherent sense of beginning or end.

At the Intercontinental Vocation Congress in Montreal in 2002 Sister Marie Chin, RSM, spoke of the aboriginal people of

Australia who have a practice of walking hundreds, sometimes thousands of miles in a year, tracking the patterns that their ancestor gods have left on the landscape as they created the world and its occupants in the mythical time known as the "Dream Time." Apparently as they walk through particular areas they sing and chant the story which describes the events that took place in Dream Time in the region through which they are passing. It seems that in recalling their deep stories people everywhere find fundamental values, beliefs, ways of acting and inspiration which give meaning to their present. Our stories hold a transformative power that touches our soul and provides a framework for belief and hope and peace in the midst of whatever fears and uncertainties may trouble us.

Religious Illiteracy

Another reality already alluded to – indeed an anomaly confronting the Catholic community – is that our young people, despite their search for God and as generous and as altruistic as ever, do not know the story of our faith and its ways of worshipping. Whether one calls it religious amnesia or illiteracy matters little. Those professors who teach the religious education courses in the faculties of education have in the past reported that very many of the Catholic students – those who intend to teach within our Catholic school system – are, in large part, religious illiterates as far as the Catholic and Christian story is concerned.

Nowhere does this illiteracy manifest itself more disturbingly that in the lack of familiarity with the centrality of the Eucharist in Catholic belief. Too many young Catholics betray a lack of any sense of the sacred and of any conceptual context within which to place the Eucharist as the centre of our Catholic life. Sacramental life is a defining characteristic of Catholic faith. It appears, however, that it is understood in very incomplete fashion by students in many of our schools. This religious illiteracy may be due in part to the failure in the schools, but it is aided and abetted when children come from families where faith is seldom celebrated, where faith is attributed little practical importance in the business of living.

The Challenge for Catholic Schools

These are some of the elements of the environment in which Catholic schools find themselves today. As members of a troubled Church we find ourselves in a country where many opinion makers wish to secularize all our social institutions according to an American model quite different from our Canadian experience. In our times on the one hand people everywhere give witness to a hunger for God; and on the other hand many students in Catholic schools seem to know precious little about God. They know too little of the story of our faith which speaks of the very God who has given us the life we treasure, the air we breathe and the universe in which we find ourselves. This is the paradox we live and the challenge that confronts us today in our Catholic schools.

As our society seeks a story that will provide meaning, our schools and the students within them seem, as outlined in our initial chapter, to be losing the thread of our religious story. Or perhaps we have lost the capacity to tell our story in words and ways that resonate with contemporary experience. One asks also whether we find ourselves on the verge of losing that sense of community and religious belonging which is the medium, the context within which the story can be ever told anew. This is the threat from within and the challenge we face. It is a threat that challenges the Catholic educational partners to achieve consensus and commitment on how to deal with it if we are to move successfully in this 21st century.

The challenge which we face is, therefore, twofold. As indicated in the previous chapter we must find the words and the ways and the symbols to tell our Christian story so that it will resonate with the experience, the search and the desires of both the parents and the kids in our schools. The challenge is to announce anew and in contemporary fashion the Christian and Catholic answer to the perennial search for our souls. The challenge is to articulate anew the myth, the narrative which has given hope and meaning and coherence to the Christian journey of our forbears.

The second part of the challenge is to create, in our highly individualistic society, the Christian community which is essential to the telling of the story. To know the story and to have it affect our lives requires that we be part of a community which has created and continues to create this story. For it is the community which gives flesh and blood to the story. It is the community which clothes the story in contemporary garments and thereby makes it comprehensible to succeeding generations.

I would not hesitate to suggest that this challenge is of such importance that all partners in our Catholic school system in consensual fashion must make of it the fundamental and distinctive goal according to which we will measure the success or failure of our schools in the days ahead.

If together we can commit to this, we should be assured that there is no reason to believe that we are presiding at a death watch. Ultimately this is a challenge not just for the school system but for the whole Church. Catholic schools are uniquely positioned to respond to this new challenge. We cannot ignore the fact that more Catholics touch the life of the church at the level of the school than at the level of parish and diocese. The incredible resource our school system represents within our Church in Ontario sometimes seems to remain a hidden treasure. We have a school system which is well if not adequately funded to the tune of more than $5 billion annually. More importantly we have 36,000 well-trained teachers, who are substantially committed and dedicated to the mission of Catholic schools. There are as well hundreds of trustees who give unstintingly of their time and talents in search of further developing our Catholic education system. Parents, school councils, parishes and parish councils in their different ways complete the triad on which Catholic education has traditionally been built.

None of these people is perfect. But the story of our faith, our sacred writings, tell us that those called by God have seldom been perfect. The Peters and Pauls, the Isaiahs and Moses, the Martin Luther Kings and Mother Teresas have all been flawed and wounded human beings. They were people who often with some reluctance recognized, the disruptive call of

God as it breaks into ordinary lives and asks ordinary people to assume the extraordinary mission of human transformation. Our hope rests with these ordinary people to pick up the challenge and achieve these two fundamental goals of telling our story anew and of creating the learning environment of Christian community in which it must be told.

Telling the Story Throughout the Curriculum

To consciously and intentionally hand on a heritage and tradition, a history and a way of living, and an anthropology which tells us who we are, entails more than courses in religious education. It involves educating young baptized Catholics within a philosophy and context of learning in which all curriculum, all subjects and disciplines are inspired and informed by the faith story recounted in our sacred writings and tradition. Ours is an understanding of learning and teaching, ours is a philosophy of education founded on the conviction that the sacred and the secular are ever related one to the other. Our approach to education is grounded in assuring that the well-educated graduate of a Catholic school system will be equipped to make the connections in life between the wonders of the physical universe, the beauty of the arts, the magic of language and that mystery of life who is our God. This approach is well articulated in the document from the Institute for Catholic Education (ICE) entitled "Ontario Catholic School Graduate Expectations."

This is what is distinctive in Catholic curriculum. It reflects a shared conviction that there are no neutral economics, or literature, or drama or hard or soft sciences courses in Catholic school programs. The story we tell has meaning for all subjects and disciplines and implications for all of life.

Catholic educators do not pretend that this approach to education occurs in some kind of social and cultural vacuum. With the wide variety of value systems, ideologies, stories and world views which compete every day for the attention and even the commitment of young people, with so many families living a life of practical atheism, Catholic educators are in no way assured of winning the Christian commitment of all students. Catholic schools should, however, recognize a fundamental responsibility, a primary purpose. This fundamental responsibility is that their graduates in all disciplines and other curricular experiences will be taught the story, the tradition, the moral code and the ways of prayer and worship of those people who throughout the centuries have followed the meaning of life as revealed in the Good News of Jesus Christ. In making known to our students the rich heritage of the Christian faith our hope is that they reach out and grasp this message as a way of life and apply it to all dimensions and experiences of their human journey.

The measurable goal is that they be taught and come to know this story and heritage. That they will believe in it and commit their lives to the Christian way happens only in the mystery of God's gift of faith.

Telling Our Story with New Language

Catholic educators daily confronted with the reality of varying degrees of religious illiteracy among students face another challenge. They are also confronted with the need to help students – and themselves – integrate the world view of a technological and scientific society with their belief. Few Catholic educators have not realized that our language, our words, our teaching, do not seem to have the power to communicate that they once possessed. More is involved than children not knowing our tradition and heritage. Mention has already been made of the urgent need for new words, for a new language – a language which resonates with contemporary experience and communicates with the present generations. The marvellous and mind-shattering advances in science in the past century have meant that our world view, our cosmology, is profoundly different from the world view and cosmology of previous generations. Our deepened understanding of historical context and how it conditions everything from theological concepts, to scientific understanding, to artistic expression, to history itself, has resulted in our contemporaries thinking differently and expressing themselves differently. There has been a profoundly radical shift in how we grasp and in how we speak of life itself, the human journey and the physical and moral universe in which we find ourselves.

Vaclav Havel, the former Czech president, but also the prophet and poet of the Czechoslovakian revolution, in speaking of our present times has said, "Today, many things indicate that we are going through a transitional period, when it seems that something is on its way out and something else is being painfully born. It is as if something were crumbling, decaying, and exhausting itself, while something else, still indistinct, were arising from the rubble." It is not surprising that often the very words and concepts of our faith often seem to have been hollowed out, to have lost their transforming power.

In this context it is helpful to remember just how significantly the words we use lose or change their meaning. Someone wrote recently that not too long ago:

• a chip meant a piece of wood, hardware meant hardware, and software wasn't even a word;

• fast food was what you ate in Lent;

• bunnies were small white rabbits and rabbits weren't Volkswagens;

• and grass was something you mowed and Coke was something you drank.

Only in recent years has it been clearly borne in upon us that a radical rearticulating or re-speaking of the faith is necessary. It serves no purpose simply to shout louder with a language that is foreign to the ears of our contemporaries, be they our young people or their parents.

Much of the impetus and challenge which occasioned the Second Vatican Council came from the recognized need to more fittingly engage our world in dialogue – a dialogue which would more clearly reveal the aspirations of modern men and women to the Church and again reveal the message of the gospel for the people of modernity. At the opening of this Ecumenical Council Pope John XXIII obviously sensed the new moment which humanity is living. He told us that although the eternal and essential truths of our faith remain ever the same they must effectively be clothed in and expressed in new words, new concepts, in a new language, if they are to touch and affect the lives of contemporary men and women.

The great German theologian Karl Rahner expressed the same conviction:

> *The form of preaching (teaching) in a particular age must be "translated" into another form of preaching (teaching) to make the language understood, particularly if the meaning of the message must remain the same. This preservation of identity cannot be achieved by the mere repetition of old expressions if the mentality and concepts change in secular society through an historical development which is not under the Church's control.* ("Demythologization and the Sermon" in *The Renewal of Preaching: Theory and Practice,* Concilium 33, 1968)

So we need new words, a new language. The lexicon of this new language will include the mind-boggling discoveries of the physicist and of the astronomer, the vocabulary of information technology and the marvels of evolution and of genetic engineering. More importantly the accent of our language, the distinctiveness of our language must bespeak care and compassion, conversion, prayer, beauty and inclusiveness.

A Language of Care and Compassion

As Catholics seek to discover the proper new words to express the age old traditions and teaching of our faith, as we struggle with the language of the new orthodoxy, we must speak more loudly than ever that language of human care and concern that beats at the heart of the gospel. Our schools within the classrooms, at the board table, and in all the many relationships involved in a school system must be seen to reflect not so much the commandments or the imperatives of our tradition as the beatitudes of the gospel. If the language of orthodoxy is once again in the making, the language of orthopraxis – of doing what the gospel calls us to – remains ever clear. The words of our new language most importantly will be words expressed through the medium of social justice, of compassion, care and commitment seeking always to express the reality of a God of love. Perhaps in our present climate it is this language which will best be understood, especially with our secondary school students. Interestingly, even the secular world which often flinched at the religious words and theology of Mother Teresa was profoundly moved by the words which her actions bespoke. One hopes that this language of Christian orthopraxis can lead us anew to the language of prayer as mentioned below.

A Language of Conversion

In assuring that our story and its teachings, beliefs and moral codes be told in clear and uncompromising fashion in all of our schools we cannot ignore the fact that so many of our kids come from non-practising families. As they enter a Catholic school classroom many of them can hardly be called believers. If they are not believers then we should speak not a language of catechesis but of conversion. This has consequences for how we teach in Catholic schools and how we develop our catechetical programs.

The starting point is recognizing that a search for meaning, for God, for something that transcends ourselves is part of the experience of all students. In a world in which students ricochet from pillar to post among competing values, young people, indeed all of us, sense the need for some consistent worldview, something that will make sense out of death and the moral ambiguities that all face. The Catholic story is about the wonder and dignity of each of us, created by God and held in His hand. So we must tell young people above all else that they are good and great and worthwhile. Young people want to hear that message even though they may not realize how much they want to hear it. Psychologists in giving advice to parents whose young children were traumatized by the events of September 11, 2001, suggested that above all they should hug them and hold them.

This is the kind of precious zone of personal stability which a Catholic school should offer. Students need a place where there is some coherence. In this space which allows for the quiet of their own souls Catholic educators let young people grapple with the questions and the value systems which compete for their attention. If we create this coherent and consistent zone of stability, then we can offer a contemporary *kerygma,* a simple statement of the essential message of the gospel and pray that the students will be converted to it.

A Language of Prayer

The language of prayer in its own mysterious way seems to communicate with us all. It is not too much to say that our schools shoud teach a language of contemplation. Contemplation has been described as "... a gracious act of waking up, taking notice of, paying attention, and becoming alive to time, place and the world around us. It is engaging God who is present in the here and now" (Sr. Marie Chin). Surely it was to this contemplative approach that John Paul II was referring when addressing educators in Newfoundland in 1984. Catholic educators, he said, "... must grasp firmly the challenge of providing a kind of education whose curriculum must be inspired more by reflection than by technique, more by the search for wisdom than the accumulation of information."

Our Catholic tradition offers many different ways and paths that lead one into the life of prayer. Ignatian, Teresian and Benedictine spiritualities are but parts of our rich heritage. Of particular importance is that prayer of mysticism that brings together, unites one with and immerses one in the wonder of all life, the marvel of the entire universe, and the mystery of a creating God. This mystical tradition finds echo in today's ecological and environmental concerns as well as in the search for some meaning that transcends the all-consuming materialism which so reduces us. Centred in the quietness of God, our prayer traditions resonate with the words of the Indian poet and philosopher, Rabindranath Tagore: "The same stream of life that runs through my veins night and day runs through the world and dances in rhythmic measures."

Catholic schools should provide an atmosphere which naturally leads and teaches children to pray. Amidst the din of cell phones and iPods never before has the quiet of prayer been so essential to maintain individual faith as in our increasingly secular society. Forms of prayer such as centring prayer provide a sense of inner peacefulness. That prayer which gives permission to the imagination would best be taught to young people before their religious imagination is in some way atrophied by the secularism of our times.

A Language of Esthetics

The language of our narrative will also be a language which finds expression through the arts and all the cultural riches of both our tradition and contemporary society. Recently Liona Boyd, the Canadian classical guitarist, quoted the German poet and dramatist Johann Goethe. He once said: "A person should hear a little music, read a little poetry and see a live picture every day in order that worldly cares may not obliterate the sense of the beautiful which God has implanted in the human soul" (*Globe and Mail*, May 4, 2002).

Our words must allow for the wonder and the awe which beauty inspires. Our curriculum must be as much about appreciation as about information - appreciation for the miracle of life and the universe in which we live. Toward the end of his life the great American rabbi Abraham Joshua Heschel in the preface to his book of Yiddish poems wrote, "I did not ask for success: I asked for wonder. And you gave it to me." Some years ago the American priest sociologist and novelist, Andrew Greeley, called for a new approach to the way in which we tell our story in Catholic schools. His prescription is that we should emphasize what is beautiful in our story and in sound doctrine: "At every step of the educational process we must attend to beauty — that small tear in the surface of the world, as Simone Weil puts it, that pulls us through to some vaster space. Beauty lifts us off the ground, spins us around and then deposits us back on the ground perhaps only a few inches away. It is not that we no longer stand at the centre of the world; we never did. Rather, we are still in the power of that which has happened to us in our encounter with beauty. But encounters with beauty open us up to their own alchemy, which gently guides us to goodness and truth" (*America*, Sept. 16, 2000).

A Language of Inclusiveness

Our new language will be such that it renders no one invisible. In the language of all subjects but perhaps particularly in religion the language of a Catholic school will recognize the power of words to include and empower, or to exclude and make invisible. The sometimes rigorously masculine language of our tradition will be modified so as to bring all into its expression. In the use of language we shall make our own the wisdom of the American poet Maya Angelou, "We did what we knew how to do, and when we knew better, we did better."

Creating the Learning Environment of Christian Community

A second fundamental goal or objective of a Catholic school is to assure that students are exposed not only to the notions, ideas, words and language of Christian faith, but to the experience of people striving and indeed struggling to follow in a secular society this way of life, this journey, as revealed in the gospel story. In other words consensual commitment to the creation of the unique learning environment of Christian community within the school is needed as a privileged objective. This will be a basic criterion in determining whether we are being effective in the delivery of Catholic education. Community in the Catholic theological tradition is the primary *locus revelationis* – the primary place where God speaks to us and reveals his face to us. Creating community is not accidental to the Catholic educational enterprise but at the very heart of what we do.

There is a visceral realization in Catholic practice that the living out of our faith is never a flight of the alone to the Alone. For Catholics moments of deep meaning, of birth and baptism, of love and marriage, of the meal of Eucharist, and of death and dying, are not moments to be lived alone. They are moments to be lived with one another. Community may be a reality that is difficult to define – but usually it is easy to recognize.

For some people in our society it is little more than a social construct – a grouping of people coming together simply to realize an achievable goal. More thoughtfully, however, others such as the late spiritual writer Henri Nouwen have recognized that "community is created when we care for the vulnerable." Community is created when not only a school staff but also those who support the school recognize that in some way we are jointly responsible for our children, a unique group of vulnerable people. They have been entrusted to us; and we must realize that we are responsible through community to offer life-meaning to these very vulnerable, mysterious and precious human beings who are our children.

It is not easy to be a community person today. All involved in Catholic education, like many believers today are tempted to go it alone in their quest for God. It is part of the individualism of our times. The temptation may be particularly strong as our Roman Catholic community is confronted with the sins of the clergy, with the unpopularity of our social justice teaching and the political incorrectness of opposing things like abortion and euthanasia. In all of this we might listen with profit to the same Henri Nouwen, who despite his own problems with the Church, had this to say:

> *First of all, listen to the Church. I know that isn't a popular bit of advice at a time and in a country where the Church is frequently seen more as an "obstacle" in the way rather than as the 'way' to Jesus. Nevertheless, I'm profoundly convinced that the greatest spiritual danger of our times is the separation of Jesus from the Church. The Church is the body of the Lord. Without Jesus there can be no Church; and without the Church we cannot stay united with Jesus. I've yet to meet anyone who has come closer to Jesus by forsaking the Church. To listen to the Church is to listen to the Lord of the Church. Specifically, this means taking part in the Church's liturgical life. Advent, Christmas, Lent, Easter, Ascension, and Pentecost; these seasons and feasts teach you to know Jesus better and better, and unite you more and more intimately with the divine life he offers you in the Church.* (Nouwen, Henry J. M., *Show Me the Way: Readings for Each Day of Lent*, pp. 111-12)

It is true that there can be spirituality without formal religious practice, without community. It is true that the community's liturgy in some parishes doesn't seem to do much for our relationship with God. But to believe in our secular world we do need a community, a structure, a place to stand before God with other people struggling like ourselves with all the questions of life.

It may well be that the most important exercise or object of all professional development for both educators and trustees will be discussion concerning the ways of creating community. This should surely be the principal objective of every school principal and staff. They should, as well, be aided in the achievement of that objective by all of the support services for which supervisory officers are responsible.

To sum up, the fundamental goals or objectives of telling our story in contemporary language and creating the learning environment of Christian community are defining characteristics of a modern Catholic school. In the language of the day efficient and effective schools are those which achieve their stated goals and objectives. It is, therefore, the Catholic school which attains these distinctive goals which will be an efficient and effective Catholic school. The attainment of these two goals defines the particular kind of efficiency we look for in effective Catholic schools. Our second question must be to determine how the partners in Catholic education should hold themselves accountable in the attainment of these goals or purposes.

Accountability in Catholic Education

If consensus can be achieved about the importance of these fundamental goals for effective or efficient Catholic schools, our way into the future also demands that we develop some consensus around a process of accountability for their attainment.

Essential to determining the distinctive efficiency of Catholic schools will be the creation and implementation of measures or standards applicable to boards and to teachers, to students, to parents, parishes and dioceses — measures which can assess how efficient our schools are in communicating the Christian story and how efficient they are in creating Christian community. The obvious and immediate objection to this will be that these objectives are not measurable as are numeracy and literacy. The objection is that we would be trying to quantify that which is unquantifiable.

The answer to this objection is that assessment and evaluation from a Catholic education perspective cannot be reduced only to the quantifiable. To do so is to agree with an educational approach which would measure literacy and numeracy alone – and would measure them in ways that allow only for the rigidly mathematical type of evaluation which can be fed into a computer and analysed. Such is the very limited kind of evaluation which technology can provide.

There are, however, other legitimate and commonly recognized educational goals such as moral reasoning, social co-operation and other behavioural goals. These goals are found not only in the Catholic school system. The achievement of these goals is difficult if not impossible to evaluate in rigid numerical fashion, but we must evaluate them nonetheless albeit in different fashion. This, surely, is already done in what is termed "portfolio assessment" which seeks to report on many different aspects of a student's life in the school and classroom. Catholic schools with their additional and distinctive educational goals represent an enlargement of the envelope of portfolio assessment. Such evaluation can apply not only to students but to boards and teachers and the other partners in the Catholic educational enterprise.

Accountability for the Traditional Partners

Although every partner must in different ways be accountable for providing efficient Catholic education, here only the accountability of the traditional partners of schools (boards and educators), parishes/dioceses, and parents is addressed.

Accountability for Boards

If communicating the Christian story is a primary goal of Catholic education, then an indicator of an efficient Catholic school board will be its acceptance of responsibility and allocation of resources for assuring that teachers in Catholic schools have every opportunity to become knowledgeable in the Christian story and tradition, and knowledgeable in how the gospel relates to their particular disciplines or subjects. Another indicator will be the extent to which the board provides to all employees insight and technique in community-building skills so that educators especially will be as well equipped as possible to create that distinctive learning environment which is the community of a Catholic school.

To do this, boards must determine what recognized needs their teachers have in this regard. Then they must provide the resources necessary for whatever remediation may be necessary. In responding to whatever needs are identified the Catholic school community might introduce its own programs and procedures for assuring the constant professional updating of the teachers within its system. (Perhaps to assist in such a needs assessment the Catholic school community might consider following up on the Blishen Report which provided a snapshot of the Catholic education community in 1990. Is it not time to ask where we are today in terms of the perspective which the different partners bring to our common task?)

Another indicator for which a Catholic board should be accountable relates to the physical realities of community building. There is more than adequate research which indicates that certain school sizes effectively render the building of a school community impossible. If smaller buildings are out of the question for financial reasons it is still possible to have more than one school community within the same building. This experiment has proved quite successful within other educational jurisdictions.

For Catholic school boards to move in these directions probably means that the current funding formula needs refinement in its prescriptions as to how Catholic boards spend their dollars. This is not primarily to ask for more dollars (although such seems needed) but to impress upon the government that a distinctive school system must be distinctively funded if the constitutional guarantees for Catholic education are to be honoured. It probably means, as well, that the broader Catholic community seriously investigates whether it will financially support our schools in providing for the various programs that lend distinctiveness to the system and for which the Catholic system will not receive more dollars than the public system.

Accountability for Educators

In speaking of accountability as applied to the educators in the Catholic school system considerable enlightenment is to be found in the judicial decision of Mr. Justice Sharpe regarding the constitutionality of section 136 of the Education Act. This section, inserted into the Education Act at the time of the legislation which completed the Catholic system, took away the power of Catholic boards to discriminate in the hiring of teachers. No longer would they be able to give preference to teacher applicants who shared the Catholic faith. The section was successfully challenged by the Ontario Catholic School Trustees' Association. In his 1998 ruling regarding this matter Justice Sharpe underlined and emphasized the centrality of the teacher to the Catholic educational process. In support of his decision he quoted the Supreme Court of Canada which said, "The religious or doctrinal aspect of the school lies at its very heart and colours all its activities and programs. The role of the teacher in this respect is fundamental to the whole effort of the school, as much in its spiritual nature as in the academic" (Daly and the Attorney General of Ontario at p. 41).

The secular courts of our land have recognized that Catholic education ultimately will rise or fall on the commitment, the competence and the dedication of its teachers. Anyone involved in education knows that after all the theory, all the administrative procedures, all the financial support, education achieves it goals or fails to do so when the classroom door closes and teachers interact with their students. The heart of Catholic education will always be its teachers. And in Catholic schools the story of our faith and the sense of community which it engenders will only happen through the classroom teachers.

Perhaps we must ask them, as the professionals, how they would envision a process of accountability in this regard. Their association may find that this is a task for which they have no taste. If this is the case how can we turn to the teachers themselves to provide the answer to this essential question?

Accountability for Parishes/Dioceses

The present moment in the history of Catholic education is not marked by a particularly close relationship between parishes/dioceses or between priests/bishops and Catholic schools. A variety of reasons may account for this. Ever larger school administrative units over the past few decades have created not only physical but psychological distance between school and parish. Diminishing numbers of clergy and religious in the teaching profession have resulted in fewer personal bonds between different Church institutions. Fewer parish priests have meant fewer school visits by priests who in the past most often provided the link between parish and school. Rightful emerging lay responsibility has not always happened in the most felicitous of circumstances.

Some 18 years ago the bishops of Ontario spoke of the increasing importance of the Catholic school within the life of the Church in Ontario. In their well accepted pastoral letter on Catholic education they said, "Given the increasing fragility of families and the overextension of parishes, it is becoming more obvious that the school, for some (today one could say for most), is often the primary place where young people experience the Church as an alternative community..." (*This Moment of Promise*, p. 16).

More than ever, therefore, is there need to determine today the role and the responsibility parishes/dioceses have in Catholic education, and how they are to be held accountable.

If telling the story of our faith and creating a learning environment of Christian community are the crucial and distinctive goals and objectives then surely bishops as the overseers of the faith, and priests as their primary collaborators, have an essential role. The primary role of the bishop is to teach the faith along with his presbyterium, his priests. Other educational partners should expect, therefore, leadership not simply in repeating the teachings of our faith but in applying them amidst the welter of personal and social moral issues that confront the education community every day.

Such teaching requires regular contact with the other partners. What regularly scheduled meetings should take place between local bishops and school board, parent and teacher representatives? And what regularly scheduled meetings should occur between parish representatives and the other partners?

This kind of regular consultation among the partners on the provincial level produced the well informed and well received teaching of the bishops as seen in their Fully Alive series on family life and in the above-mentioned brochure *This Moment of Promise*. But should this not happen in more regular fashion in ways that would address the ever new and contemporary faith and moral questions relating to school board policy, ministry decisions, social change, bio-ethics and so on?

And if such involvement and responsibilities fall upon the shoulders of priest and bishop the next question is: How do they see themselves as being accountable to the rest of the Catholic education community in the fulfilment of these roles?

Accountability for Parents/School Councils

If there is a single obvious weakness in the legislation of the Ministry of Education regarding school councils it is that so much is expected of the latter that they are liable to be paralysed by overchoice. In their brochure Involving Other Parents: the Primary Focus of a Catholic School Council, the Catholic trustees association has suggested a way out of this dilemma. This association suggests that if school councils are primarily about improving student learning then Catholic school councils should focus on involving as many parents as possible in the education of their own kids as the best way to make this happen. The trustees put forward two major reasons for making the involvement of parents in the education of their kids a fundamental focus and priority. First of all from a theoretical perspective, Catholic education philosophy has always acknowledged parents as the primary educators of their children; and secondly research continues to pile up showing how parental involvement is of such crucial importance in improving the learning of children.

There surely are other roles for Catholic school councils as articulated in Regulation 612 of Ontario's Education Act. Catholic school councils, however, should give precedence to the task of involving as many parents as they can in the education of their own kids. As well, Catholic school councils should include in their bylaws the stated objective of assisting in the creation of a learning environment of Christian community in their schools. In so doing they would accept some responsibility for involving not only parishes but other Catholic institutions and agencies in the community education efforts of Catholic schools. These same school councils must also devise processes of accountability whereby they report back to those who elect or appoint their members. Only if the Catholic school community is commonly committed to the pursuit of the fundamental goals, objectives and purposes outlined above will there be a truly efficient Catholic system. And only an efficient Catholic system can hope to survive in the months and years ahead.

Allow me to conclude with words other than the language of efficiency and accountability. In our Christian and Catholic vocabulary we tend to speak more of promise and covenant. In our celebrations of baptism, of confirmation, of marriage and ordination our words are words of promise – of promise to one another, to the community and to God. When Catholic men and women run for the office of trustee, when teachers accept the responsibility to teach in a Catholic school they make promises to the rest of the community. They promise that they will strive to see that the young people who enter a Catholic school will enter a learning environment that is like no other, that they will experience a community where the face of God is discoverable around every corner, that in all the struggle of our human living great hope and trust and love are possible.

Thornton Wilder's play *By the Skin of Our Teeth* provides a powerful insight into the meaning of promise. In this play one of the main characters is Maggie Antrobus. Her husband, George, is running off with another woman. In the second act we hear Maggie saying this to him:

"I didn't marry you because you were perfect, George. I didn't even marry you because I loved you. I married you because you gave me a promise. That promise made up for your faults. And the promise I gave you made up for mine. Two imperfect people got married and it was that promise that made the marriage ... and when our children were growing up it wasn't the house that protected them; and it wasn't our love that protected them – it was that promise."

Teachers and trustees, and all involved in Catholic education, make promises fully aware of the weakness of our every endeavour, of the flabbiness of our human commitments. It is, however, in our ongoing struggle, in our own search and striving, that the Christian story is told and that the community of the Church, of God's people is created. When such happens we have efficient and accountable Catholic schools which will be beacons of hope for both our Church and our society.

Chapter III

Called to Teach: The Catholic Teacher as Witness

On Dec. 17, 1997, a judgment was handed down by the Ontario Court of Justice. It concerned a section of the Education Act which prevented Catholic school boards from discriminating in favour of Roman Catholics when hiring teachers. This section had been challenged as unconstitutional by the Ontario Catholic School Trustees' Association. It was declared as null and having no effect by the courts.

It is instructive to hear what a voice from "outside the box," what a voice from our secular courts has to say about the centrality of the teacher's role in the Catholic school. In overturning the section being contested this decision quoted with approval these words from an earlier court decision by Mr. Justice McIntyre: "The relationship of the teacher to the student (in a Catholic school) enables the teacher to form the mind and the attitudes of the student and the Church depends not so much on the usual form of academic instruction as on teachers who, in imitation of Christ, are required to reveal the Christian message in their work as well as in all aspects of their behaviour" (Caldwell v. Stuart, 1984, 2S.C.R. 603).

Interestingly this language is closely mirrored by the Second Vatican Council's Declaration on Christian Education which says, "But let teachers realize that to the greatest possible extent they determine whether the Catholic school can bring its goals and undertakings to fruition" (no. 8). More recently the Congregation for Catholic Education in its 1998 statement *The Catholic School on the Threshold of the Third Millennium* echoes this teaching: "... teachers and educators fulfil a specific vocation and share equally specific participation in the mission of the Church to the extent that 'it depends chiefly on them whether the Catholic school achieves its purpose'" (no. 19).

The bishops of Ontario have described teachers as "the ones involved most directly in creating the learning climate within Catholic schools" and as the ones to whose care the Church entrusts its young members (*This Moment of Promise*, p. 26).

Both our Church and our secular society recognize and acknowledge that the teacher shares in the very mission of the Church, that the teacher is at the centre and is the very heart of Catholic education. Both acknowledge that teachers hold the key to the success and future of Catholic schools. As go the teachers so will go the Catholic school system.

We live today in an era and in a province where teachers and the teaching profession have been too often criticized and even held up to ridicule. One of the great ironies of the day is that as some criticize teachers for not doing their own job of educating properly others in society expect them not only to educate but to address and respond to many of the social problems of the day. They are asked not only to be educators but social workers and surrogate parents as well. And as they are asked to fulfil these many roles not only government but many Canadians perversely question the current levels of financial support for education.

Teachers in Catholic schools face an added challenge. In our times probably only about 25 per cent of Ontario Catholics practise their faith through any visible involvement in the life of the Church. In this situation Catholic teachers are confronted with the additional challenge of more Catholics touching the life of the Church at the level of the school than at the level of the parish. It is only in the school that many Catholics brush up against and encounter the Church. So yet more is expected of the Catholic teacher.

As all of this transpires what finally to say of this profession, this call to teach, this vocation to give witness to God's truth and life and beauty?

The Meaning of Call

At the heart of most of the major religions is the belief that the mystery which is each of us is called into life itself by a gracious, creating and loving God. If the first pages of the Bible tell us anything, they tell us that not only kings and princes and rulers, but each of us is created in the image and likeness of God. Christian belief considers the human journey to be a response to and a journey of return to this continuing call of God. The message is that we are of great value. "We are here because someone wanted us to be." (Jonathan Sacks, *The Dignity of Difference*, p. 180) That each of us is also called to live out this gift of life in ways and circumstances unique to our individual human journeys is another fundamental tenet of our Judeo-Christian heritage.

We are called to live out our lives in accordance with a summons from the same God who has first given us life. We are called to give witness to the mystery of this God from whom all life flows. Although here the emphasis is upon the call of the individual it must be remembered that this is our second call. We are called first not as a gathering of isolated mystics, but as a people joined by a common life, a common calling and a common destiny with God – a people called to seek the face of God, to follow Jesus. (cf. Fr. Donald Senior at the Intercontinental Vocation Congress)

The Call of Abraham

The challenge and profound claim of God's call upon the life of the individual is evidenced nowhere more clearly than in the call of Abraham, the father in faith of our Judeo-Christian tradition. The story of Abraham, the patriarch of the Hebrew people, is about a man called by God to go into the unknown trusting in Yahweh to be with him always. In the book of Genesis we hear God call, "Leave your country, your family, and your father's house, for the land I will show you." The promise made to Abraham if he follow God's summons: "I will make you a great nation; I will bless you and make your name so famous that it will be used as a blessing" (Gen. 12:1-2).

Abraham was in effect called to leave everything that he knew, everything he was comfortable with, everything he was in control of, and emigrate to a foreign land. Abraham was a nomad, in all probability moving his flocks within a defined area. In his own territory he knew where the best grazing lands were to be found in the different seasons. He knew where the watering holes were to be found and when they would have water. He was surrounded by the security of family. He knew who was friend and who was foe. He was in control of his life. All of this Abraham was called to leave and go into a new land, into the unknown where he would not know where grazing land and water were to be found, who was friend and who was foe, and how the seasons would unfold. He surrendered all of his certainties and securities to the God who called him. And God promised him that all would be well, indeed better than before; and he promised to be faithful to God. This covenant between God and an individual seems to mark all the great calls, all the great vocations, in the Bible.

The Christian Vocation

Like Abraham every Christian has then a particular vocation or call to fulfil the destiny which is his or hers as a singular and unique mystery in the unfolding of God's universe. In the life of those who in the Spirit follow the way of Jesus together – in the life of the Church – some of these calls or vocations are meant as a special way of service or ministry to us all. They are meant to provide a unique witness to the message and the way of the gospel.

The earliest records of the life of the early Church reveal a people who recognized that different members of their community were called by God to serve them, to care for them, to minister to them in a variety of ways. The letters of Paul give particular evidence of individuals gifted by God to accomplish a variety of ministries. In I Corinthians Paul tells this small group of believers, "Now you together are Christ's body; but each of you is a different part of it. In the Church God has given the first place to the apostles, the second to prophets, the third to teachers; after them, miracles, and after them the gift of healing; helpers, good leaders, those with many languages" (I Cor. 12:27-28). In the letter to the Romans he says, "Our gifts differ according to the grace given us. If your gift is prophecy, then use it as your faith suggests; if administration, then use it for administration; if teaching, then use it for teaching. Let the preachers deliver sermons, the almsgivers give freely, the officials be diligent, and those who do works of mercy do them cheerfully" (Rom. 12:6-8). And in Ephesians we hear, "And to some His gift was that they should be apostles; to some prophets, to some evangelists; to some pastors and teachers ..." (Eph. 4:11).

The Vocation of the Laity

Our Catholic tradition over the centuries has always recognized and celebrated this mystery of vocation. The emphasis for many years was often upon vocations to the religious life and to the priesthood. But in the early Church and recently, particularly following upon the teaching of the Second Vatican Council, increasing emphasis has been placed upon the vocation of the laity and on certain vocations through which lay persons in a particular way serve the Church and society. An article in *America* magazine (March 10, 2003) speaks of the history of the vocation of the laity. It highlights the lives of Priscilla and her husband Aquila, two great Christians who are mentioned at least four times in the New Testament. They were expelled from Rome during the persecution of Claudius, became missionary companions of the Apostle Paul in Ephesus and risked their lives for his sake and for the sake of the gospel.

If this vocation of the laity simmered on the back burner for too many years it remains within this ancient tradition that the words of Vatican II must be situated when it says, "The holy People of God shares ... in Christ's prophetic office," and when it tells us that every lay person is called to "witness to Him, especially by means of a life of faith and charity and by offering to God a sacrifice of praise" (*Lumen Gentium*, no. 12). What is clear is that in the early Church and in our own time long before there were shortages of priests and religious sisters and brothers in Catholic schools the Vatican II documents on the nature of the Church and on the role of the laity underlined the special calls or vocations of teachers.

However, despite this teaching old and new it is less than clear that our Catholic community and all Catholic teachers understand the distinctive vocation of the teacher in a Catholic school. How common and how deep is the conviction that Catholic teachers exercise their profession first and foremost not because they have the requisite degrees, not because they have been recognized b y the Ontario College of Teachers, not because they have been hired by a Catholic school board, but in virtue of a special call from God?

The Vocation of the Teacher

The documents that followed Vatican II gave clear profile to the role or vocation of every educator, Catholic, Christian, believer or non-believer. So every teacher in every school public or Catholic or whatever is not simply a professional responsible for the systematic transmission of certain bodies of knowledge. Rather, according to our tradition, the profession is described as one of responsibility within the school for the integral human formation of young people.

Our Catholic community understands this task of every teacher as striving in the community of the school "to develop persons who are responsible and inner-directed, capable of choosing freely in conformity with their conscience" (*The Catholic School*, no. 31). And of preparing these children "to open themselves up to life as it is and to create in themselves a definite attitude to life as it should be" (ibid.). Further, the school must "stimulate the pupil to exercise his intelligence through the dynamics of understanding to attain clarity and inventiveness. It must help her spell out the meaning of her experiences and their truths" (ibid., no. 27). So important is this task of stimulating the analytical thinking and creativity of the student that this same document concludes, "Any school which neglects this duty and which offers merely precast conclusions hinders the personal development of its pupils" (ibid.). In these words one hears echoes of radical opposition to any educational policy or practice which necessitates "teaching to the test."

The Vocation of the Catholic Teacher

This is the profession of all teachers whether Catholic or non-Catholic, whether lay, religious or priest. What then is specific in the call or vocation of the lay Catholic teacher? The foundational document on the nature and meaning of the Church which issued from Vatican II insisted that all the baptized are "... made sharers in the priestly, prophetic, and kingly functions of Christ. They carry out their own part in the mission of the whole Christian people with respect to the Church and the world" (*Lumen Gentium*, no. 31). Catholics who teach, however, are identified as sharing a special calling wherever they practise their profession. For the purpose of our discussion here the focus is upon the vocation of the Catholic teacher in the Catholic school.

If the integral formation of the human person is the professional responsibility of all educators; if this includes the fullest development of all that is human; if this is all about assisting human persons, especially the young, to develop their intellectual, affective and creative potential; if it means helping them to become inner-directed and capable of choosing freely in conformity with their conscience; if a teacher is called to recognize and communicate the dignity and rights of the human person and a sense of human solidarity throughout this world of ours – if all of this is the task of every teacher, then it will be our understanding of who the human person is and what this world of ours is that will ultimately distinguish one teacher from another. How Catholic teachers regard students and the world of their students should be what distinguishes them.

Educators often wonder these days why their profession seems to have been downgraded in the eyes of many. There are probably a variety of reasons explaining this phenomenon. Central to these reasons must be included how contemporary society views the world around us and the human person especially the student. If students, society and the world are regarded in wholly material and utilitarian terms – as necessary but dispensable ciphers or cogs in a consumption driven economy – then the whole educational project takes on a certain coloration and value. If, however, students and their world have, as well, a transcendent and spiritual dimension then the task of education is regarded differently. Our anthropology and indeed our cosmology play a significant role in how education is considered and how it is valued.

Contemporary World Views

In the deconstructed world of postmodernism, for many of our contemporaries much of the grandeur, the dignity and the purpose of each human being – of every student – is reduced to quantifiable units with predetermined purposes. For example, many socio-biologists consider the human organism as simply the most sophisticated of living organisms explainable totally in terms of a fundamental drive of all living organisms to preserve and pass on their DNA. For the chemist we are the $67 or the $167 or $167,000 worth of minerals and other elements which make up the human body. Perhaps most importantly is the too prevalent economic mindset that regards the human person in terms of units of production and consumption. When this latter concept prevails, when the Conference Board of Canada, the Chamber of Commerce and the Board of Trade have undue influence on schools, then education is all about a healthy economy. In this atmosphere not surprisingly many of our politicians concern themselves only with the technical and practical applications of education to the detriment of a truly liberal education. Many educational planners obsess over quantifiable test results for both student and teacher. Method and best practices become everything. The how of education takes centre stage, the why gets a walk-on role, and the who gets little attention at all as the educational drama plays itself out. As a member of Ontario's Royal Commission of Learning some eight or nine years ago I had the privilege of working with a group of intelligent and dedicated individuals. Unfortunately in the early days of our discussions together the idea of casting our work within a conceptual framework with a clear indication of who the student is and where he/she is going was discarded as it was evident that in our group there was little consensus on what human life was finally about.

The way we regard life and the destiny of the human person has profound implications for schools and for how we teach. Shakespeare was often prescient. The words of the main protagonist in his play *Macbeth* seem to intuit the way many regard human life today:

Life's but a walking shadow, a poor player
That struts and frets his hour upon the stage
And then is heard no more: it is a tale
Told by an idiot, full of sound and fury,
Signifying nothing.

In the theatre of the absurd the character Hamm appears onstage in Samuel Beckett's play *Endgame*. Peering out nervously from an ashcan with a lid on his head he hesitantly asks, "We're not starting to mean – to mean something?"

The world views shared by many of our contemporaries dictate much of the at least implicit and unexamined educational philosophy that surrounds us. It has significant influence on how some would see their profession. Education always involves at least an unconscious conceptual framework in which we place life and the human person.

The school has always been a place of intersection between the world view of teachers and the problems which beset society. At this restless moment which marks the beginning of a millennium, one of the great problems is a pervasive determinism and reductionism and in some cases a nihilism that effectively minimizes the greatness and wonder of human life. When we are told that much if not all of what we do is determined by the genes we have inherited or the environment in which we grew up, when we are consistently told that the need for a certain level of affluence determines how we live as families, when our political leaders make the economy the final arbiter of policy making (It's the economy, stupid!), when the mystery of human sexuality is reduced to selling beer and fast cars – when all this is the consistent message of the dominant culture, we are being fed a view and understanding of the human person which ends up diminishing us.

This reductionist and deterministic framework unfortunately is the conceptual framework of many of our contemporaries. It results in a narrow approach to education and a narrow understanding of the teaching profession. This is the approach that leads to almost obsessive concern with measurable or quantifiable results. These results or test scores are often more about getting ahead for both student and teacher than about integral human growth and development.

When all of this happens there is little sense of the human person as a unique mystery coming from the hand of a creating and loving God. There is little talk of the quest for the truth of ourselves and of our life, what true human freedom is, and what happens to the weak in a competitive and conflictual society such as ours.

The Student

And where is the student in this world view? What is the thinking and the attitude of those marvellous young people who come each day into our schools? Are we respecting and nourishing the enthusiasm and idealism which will ever be the gift of youth to the rest of us?

Allen Bloom in the opening chapter of his book *The Closing of the American Mind*, claims that one thing every university professor can be absolutely certain of is that "almost every student entering the university believes, or says he believes, that truth is relative ..." For today's young people, he says, "Relativism is necessary to openness; and this is the virtue, the only virtue which all primary education for 50 years has dedicated itself to inculcating." "The true believer," he adds, "is the real danger. The study of history and of culture teaches that all the world was mad in the past.... The point is not to correct the mistakes and really be right; rather it is not to think you are right at all" (pp. 25-26).

In the moral field this relativism translates into young people who make a virtue out of never judging the actions of their peers as long as such actions don't affect them personally. For the moral dimension of their own activity they rely on how it feels for them in this or that particular situation. They do not seem to have the intellectual apparatus to frame an argument as to what is good or bad for themselves, others and the community. Their moral processes seem to be little more than what the American theologian George Weigel calls "emotivism."

The Congregation for Catholic Education talks about students today who often seem incapable of self-sacrifice and perseverance – students who are "not only indifferent and non-practising, but also totally lacking in religious formation" *(The Catholic School on the Threshold of the Third Millennium,* no. 6).

Today's teachers are everywhere confronted by students immersed in a culture which most often – especially through the media – disturbingly reflects the attainment of success measured wholly in material terms. Like the perennially favourite program *Seinfeld* they are tempted to succumb to a view that ultimately life is about nothing. Confronted with such challenges Catholic teachers are called to examine and think through their own anthropology, their own cosmology, their own world view.

The World View of the Catholic Teacher

The anthropology, how the teacher understands the nature and purpose of human life and the human person, and the cosmology, how the teacher regards the universe in which we live, determine the way in which each teacher approaches his/her profession. If the wonderful, fragile and developing human lives entrusted to a teacher's care are seen as a capability, a possibility and a promise of greatness called into life and destined to return to God, then the vocation of the Catholic teacher will ever be unique. It will be inspired by a world view which demands involvement in the struggle of human life and an openness to the God revealed in Jesus Christ.

The vocation of the Catholic teacher and the *raison d'etre* of the Catholic school are rooted ultimately in the meaning of the human person and the meaning of this universe of ours as revealed by both faith and reason. Our tradition makes clear that to understand a Catholic school is to grasp that our God-given gifts of knowing and understanding, of loving and creating find their ultimate meaning in Jesus Christ. His message is the foundation on which it all rests. It is the Good News of the gospel that speaks to the ultimate destiny of every man and woman and to the meaning of destiny within the mystery of our universe. The beatitudes speak to the way of living that leads to happiness. This is the coherent and consistent learning environment in which students are encouraged to discover and search out the purpose and the path in this mystery which is human life as the crown of creation.

A Synthesis of Culture and Faith, a Synthesis of Faith and Life

To put it in other words, Catholic teaching speaks of the Catholic teacher as one responsible in a special way for helping young people look at the world or culture in which they live through the wonder and power of human understanding, imagination, creativity and through the eyes of faith; and further of assisting them to see how this knowing, imagining and believing should influence the way they live.

The document *The Catholic School*, puts it this way: "If, like every other school, the Catholic school has as its aim the critical communication of human culture and the total formation of the individual, it works toward this goal guided by its Christian vision of reality ..." (no. 36). This means bringing together the culture or world we live in and the faith we live by. Catholic education has been described as the educational attempt to enable students to develop a "synthesis of culture and faith, and a synthesis of faith and life" (ibid., no. 37). As in every education system this aim, purpose, and goal of a Catholic school depends not as much on subject matter or methodology as on the people who work there, on the teachers (ibid., no. 43).

The unique vocation of Catholic teachers then is to give witness as people who constantly examine the culture that surrounds them and its effect upon their own personal life, their professional life, and their faith life. In our own moment of history this suggests that the vocation of Catholic teachers calls them in a very special way to speak a language that in all subjects and disciplines, in all dimensions of curriculum gives witness to three fundamental Christian concerns: i) a critical quest for truth, ii) the unfettered freedom of the gospel, and iii) a community caring for the marginalized.

A Critical Quest for Truth

Francis Bacon's essay *On Truth* begins, "What is truth said jesting Pilate and would not stay for an answer." "What is truth?" is the cynical Pilate's reply to the words of Jesus Christ, "For this was I born and for this I have come into the world, to bear witness to the truth" (John 18:37). "What is truth?" is a question for our time.

In our wired world we receive massive amounts of information — too much indeed to digest. Large swaths of it unfortunately are not true. The majority of the information from the advertising world with which we are daily bombarded is meant not to inform us but to so seduce us that our wants become our needs. Often information from the various levels of government about the pillars of our society such as health care, education and social welfare, is meant to cause us to take our eye off the ball so we will not notice what is really happening. Government opposition both formal and informal so "spins" its own negative criticisms that truth is again victimized.

The democracy which we so highly prize in our western societies rests on the premise and demands that citizens be honestly informed of where their governments propose to lead them and the true reasons for such directions and policies. Deprived of such guarantees of truth, democracy is crippled and under the guise of democracy different forms of quasi-dictatorship easily take over.

In the United States for many months during the war in Iraq it was clear from most of the news programs and from surveys on the attitudes of Americans that they had been convinced by the administration of the truth of the position that not only was a pre-emptive strike against Iraq necessary but that it was morally good. Despite the statements by the National Council of Churches, representing the leadership of most of the Protestant congregations, despite the teaching of the American bishops through the United States Catholic Conference, and despite the overt opposition of Pope John Paul II, most Americans, including Roman Catholics, believed the war was morally justifiable. It was a clear example of the old maxim that "the first casualty of war is the truth."

In a more general way much of western society excludes the religious perspective from any serious discussion of economic development and policy making. Recent studies by Canada's International Development Research Centre have shown that most of the rest of the world does not share this conviction; and that economic development in their countries cannot proceed effectively without the faith convictions of their citizens being part of the process. Religious truth is still considered an essential part of true human development by many in the developing countries, but this religious truth is increasingly excluded from public policy debate in our own country.

Our times confront young people and us all with limitless possibilities, opinions and a plethora of values that have us ricocheting from pillar to post. Like Pilate, the temptation is to respond with cynicism instead of pursuing in all of this the quest for the truth. Students should be aware of how often the supposed search for truth, economic or otherwise, is dictated by assumptions and secular mindsets that distort reality. Students must have the opportunity to realize that the religious perspective, the faith perspective, is fundamental to any search for the total truth whether the matter under discussion is politics, science, economics or whatever.

In these times there is heightened reason for all of us to be seekers of the truth. Perhaps most importantly students must be given the opportunity to learn that there is truth. The so-called "hermeneutic of suspicion," the attitude of absolute skepticism about everything that often affects the academic world, must not be part of the atmosphere of enquiry of the

Catholic school. The religious perspective changes the fundamental angle of vision. The language of a Catholic school must echo a commitment to the truth. Catholic teachers are called to give witness to this perspective of searching for the truth as a believer. This concern for truth will be developed further in the final chapter.

The Freedom of the Gospel

There are few today who are not affected by the many, often unrecognized, constraints on our human freedom. It is difficult to realize at times just how "unfree" many of us are. The spiritual writer Henri Nouwen spoke often of how constrained and limited we are by the fears that surround us. We fear not only death and sickness, not only SARS and AIDS, but job loss and poverty. We are afraid of terrorists, the disapproval of others in the present, of how we look, of how the past is affecting us and of what the future may hold. In some instances we are effectively paralysed by these fears. Financial freedom is touted as the only escape from these fears. "Freedom 55" is the answer.

At times it is our insecurities that can gradually freeze our aspirations, particularly in our relationships with others and even in our relationship with God. Our society holds out impossible models, particularly to young people, suggesting that only Britney Spears and Brad Pitt look-a-likes are socially acceptable. Such models induce little idealism and much insecurity. It is little wonder that many are so bound up by a sense of slavery to what Mary Jo Leddy calls "perpetual dissatisfaction" in her book *Radical Gratitude.*

As well, there is abroad today a pervasive sense of an inevitability that appears to constrain our freedom in many different spheres. Whether talking about robotics, global economics, technology, fetus selection, the decline of the power of labour unions, or contemporary sexual mores, many appear to believe that important directions of current political, economic and ethical life are moving with a momentum that is absolutely irreversible. The accepted wisdom is that these trends or directions represent a fixed course over which humankind and its various societies have no control. The future and the human prospect are fatalistically regarded as captive to evolutionary forces which can no more be redirected or turned back than can the orbits of the planets or the tides of the oceans.

For example, many economists seem resigned to the development of a new global economy shaped by ever more sophisticated technologies and beyond any effective control of national governments. This new economy, we are told, will eventually reduce the work force to a cadre of highly skilled technocrats or experts in technology. The new "hewers of wood and carriers of water" will be huge masses of well-enough educated but technologically unsophisticated workers. These drones, if they have work at all, will require only rudimentary computer and technological literacy to labour in the service industries. They will benefit from little of the protection of organized labour and share few of the immense profits from the industries in which they work. The result will be a pear-shaped economy, both locally and globally, in which the extremely high paid "techie" will stand above and apart from the mass of drones condemned to menial, mind-numbing tasks — or to some form of unemployment sustained by minimal social assistance.

The American economist Robert Reich describes these "techies" as "symbolic analysts." Among them he includes all who control and direct the manipulation of information. Of them and of the unfortunate rest he writes:

> *Distinguished from the rest of the population by their global linkages, good schools, comfortable lifestyles, excellent health care, and abundance of security guards, symbolic analysts will complete their secession from the union. The townships and urban enclaves where they reside, and the symbolic-analytic zones where they work, will bear no resemblance to the rest of America; nor will there be any direct connections between the two. America's poorest citizens, meanwhile, will be isolated within their own enclaves of urban and rural desperation; an ever-larger proportion of their young men will fill the nation's prisons.* (*The Work of Nations*, 1991, pp. 302-03)

Already thoughtful young people express their dread of

this future which will condemn most of them to the waste heap of human productivity and creativity. They are not reassured to be told blithely that such a development represents inevitable human progress, that it is part of the technological revolution, of the globalization of market forces, of the new information society, of the post-industrial world – whatever all that means. Nor are they comforted by the argument that the industrial revolution provided more rather than less work in western society, since the industrial and technological revolutions seem to be radically different.

Students today in Catholic schools need teachers whose language reflects the message of freedom that is central to the gospel – a language that is bound neither by fear, insecurity, dissatisfaction nor inevitability. As St. Paul said, "When Christ freed us, he meant us to remain free" (Gal. 5:1). As an essential dimension of all education teachers, as mentioned earlier, are called to develop the inner directed freedom of their students. Confronted today with all that would constrict human freedom, our teaching and our tradition give witness to a belief that we do indeed have a saviour, a redeemer – that in Jesus Christ we have one who frees us from the bonds that we cannot break by ourselves, from all that would enslave us both from within and without – from all our fears and insecurities, from all our dissatisfactions and dreaded inevitabilities – that in Jesus Christ we have the promise of healing within us the brokenness and the woundedness we cannot heal ourselves. Students need to hear this in the words and the witness of their teachers.

A Community Caring for the Marginalized

In the atmosphere of rugged individualism so admired today, perhaps the most difficult challenge to Catholic teachers is to give witness to the Christian conviction that human life is communal before it is individual. The challenge is to make the language of the school and the classroom a language that resonates with the sounds of community, of society, of social responsibility and social solidarity. In the best of our Christian and Catholic tradition our language, fashioned by a shared conviction about the common origin and common destiny of the human person, speaks easily and clearly of a common good. Such language of community suggests that we are personally, as well as professionally, accountable for the lives of others – for our students and for our fellow staff members. It is a language which stands at an oblique remove from the individualism of our time.

This language of social responsibility and human solidarity will echo not only in discussions of geography, economic and political sciences, of developing peoples and human rights. It will also be heard in the pride of place Catholic teachers give to our special education kids and how we teach the children in our schools to relate to the disadvantaged, the poor and the challenged.

The American poet Robert Frost once said that "whoever controls the words controls the world." That is why in Catholic schools a privileged hearing must be given to a voice that is catholic – a voice that is catholic or universal in that it is ever attentive to the words of the poor, of native people, of women, of the old, the young, the disabled and challenged, and of developing peoples. Our students must hear these words and not only the words of rich, middle-aged, white and healthy males.

All of this is not new. If you know the history of Catholic schools in this province you will know that from their beginnings Catholic schools offered hope to many little people. The Benedictine Sister Joan Chittister described these latter as people born bright but not rich. It was Catholic education, she claims, that made them competent and gave them confidence to make them part of a society that did not care for them all.

All teachers and all departments in a Catholic school share this responsibility. Although recognizing that there is no such thing as Catholic math or Catholic physics, Catholic teachers today, even in the so-called hard sciences, know that math and physics and all the sciences create bodies of knowledge and have research agendas which are full of value questions – and value questions are always community questions – questions whose answers either further distance the marginalized or bring them in from the cold. All of this will ensure that kids in Catholic schools come to learn there is nothing value-neutral about the specific applications of all the sciences, especially as these sciences have an effect upon how the goods of this earth are shared. The end result of this approach is that every department takes responsibility for a language of interconnectedness, of social solidarity, of community.

Young people in Catholic schools will hear and learn language that is other than what St. Augustine called the ice-cold words of "mine" and "thine." They will also know what speed skater Catriona LeMay Doan meant when she recalled the Olympic gold she brought home – and of which Canadians were so proud. She said, "My medals are a part of everybody. In 21 years of speed skating, there are so many people who were responsible for getting me to the podium." And she added, "There are many people involved in how I handle things and who I am today. A lot comes down to faith and family. They're the ones who help me stay grounded ..." (*The Catholic Register*, June 16, 2002).

The Witness of the Teacher

The vocation of the Catholic teacher finally is to give witness to his/her own faith. As the old saying goes, "The loudness of what we are doing will always drown out what we are saying." This does not mean that educators are called to plaster saint perfection. As the bishops of Ontario have said, "It is not necessary to be free of faults and failures to be faithful to the integrity of the process of Catholic education. Otherwise none of us would dare to be involved" (*This Moment of Promise*, p. 26). It does mean that teachers must be convinced that they make a difference – that their faith and their religion make a difference not only personally but globally. Institutional religion is under attack these days. Some of these attacks unfortunately are justified as when clergy abuse their position and violate young children, or when war is justified in the name of religion, or when religion sanctions the horridness of terrorism. But it is religion and our faith that have inspired much of the beauty in this world, in music and art and in the release of all that is great in the human spirit. Religion played no small part in overthrowing the oppression that under communism dominated much of Eastern Europe. Religious faith brings hope and a sense of coherence and consistence to those on the brink of despair – and for young people it can help furnish those personal zones of stability they so desperately need in our fast paced and changing world.

Catholic teachers should not fear to give witness to their faith even when it is attacked and sometimes troubled. Here in our own country, in Newfoundland in 1984 John Paul II announced to Catholic educators, "Through you, as through a clear window on a sunny day, students must come to see and know the richness and the joy of life lived in accordance with his (Christ's) teaching .... To teach means not only to impart what we know, but also to reveal who we are by living what we believe." And he continued, "By offering your students the truth of Christ you are likewise helping them to experience His freedom. You are thus engaged in the authentic liberation of this generation of students, to whom Jesus Christ, who calls Himself the 'Truth,' repeats His Gospel promise: 'If the Son makes you free, you will be free indeed'" (John 8:36).

To fulfil their vocation of giving witness to a critical search for truth, to the radical freedom of the gospel and a community committed to caring for the marginalized, Catholic teachers need the support and assistance of the whole Catholic education community, indeed the whole Church. Nowhere is this more obvious than in their need for adequate courses in faculties of education as they prepare for their future specific responsibilities in Catholic schools, and for ongoing professional development which will take account of the distinctiveness of the Catholic school system. Teachers come from the same world and hear everywhere the din of the same reductionist secular story as the rest of us. For them the Catholic community must strive to assure that they know well the story, the sacred writings, the heritage and the tradition of those people who believe in Jesus Christ. This is owed to them if the expectation is that they give witness to the faith of this community.

There will always be times, moments of difficulty and uncertainty in the Catholic teacher's vocation to witness to God's truth, the freedom of the gospel and caring community. In these moments teachers aware of and convinced of their unique vocation might make theirs the prayer of John Henry Cardinal Newman:

You have created me to do some definite service:
You have committed some work to me,
which You have not committed to another:
I have my mission –
I may never know it in this life, but I shall be told it in the next.
I am a link in a chain, a bond of connection between persons.
You have not created me for naught.
I shall do good, I shall do Your work.

(As paraphrased by Mary Jo Leddy in *Radical Gratitude*, p. 136)

Chapter IV

Catholic Education and Community Education

The lone gunslinger – John Wayne or Clint Eastwood or more recently Keanu Reeves or Jack Bauer of *24* fame – is celebrated as hero in our western society. This reflects the pervasive individualism that is a dominant characteristic of the secular society of our postmodern times. This individualism profoundly affects the image we have of ourselves and our society and has significant influence on how we do business, on our politics, on the media and even in the courts of the land. The fiction abroad is that, be it in business, or family, or personal life, or whatever, the normal and admirable way of proceeding is to pull ourselves up by our bootstraps and do it alone.

Our society seems either to be convinced or ready to maintain the pretence that all of our problems can best be solved by autonomous individuals working and competing with one another in a market economy. Within this conceptual framework it is not surprising that for many the primary educational objective has become producing graduates who will fit into this social, cultural and economic vision. This perspective considers community to be nothing but a social construct or social contract in which individual human beings come together only to realize some project that the individual alone cannot manage. Indeed some claim that the community has been replaced by the organization – and that the organization is simply a means or a tool to achieve the ends of individuals (Cf. Peter Drucker in *Atlantic Monthly*, 1994). The fiction is that if everyone looks after himself or herself all will be well in society. This is the all-encompassing and contemporary climate that renders difficult the task of Catholic schools to create Christian community as their distinctive learning environment.

The approach of individualism is absolutely foreign to Catholic self-understanding. Our teaching has always recognized that we are not only individual persons, but that by our very definition as human beings we belong to a community of persons, or several communities of persons. Christian self-understanding recognizes that there will always be some tension, some necessary dialogue between the individual person and the communities they belong to. But the heritage of Christian belief is that belonging to community is a constitutive dimension of being human. By definition the human person is a person in relation with other human persons. At its deepest level community involves a communion with all of creation, with all who have gone before us, and with the very life of God. More of this later.

Such belief finds little echo in our era. Rather, the prevalent sound of our western world is the mantra of individualism.

In his presentation to the Institute for Catholic Education symposium in 2002, Tom Reilly, then the general secretary for the Ontario Conference of Catholic Bishops, underlined three areas of practice that should identify Catholic education. The first two were academic excellence and schools recognizable for giving meaning to life and a reason for living. The third, and the one he suggested would be the most difficult of all, is the development and sustaining of a sense of community. Creating and re-creating Christian community as the distinctive learning environment of the Catholic school challenges all Catholic educators, and the Catholic Church, in this age of individualism.

Paradoxically perhaps, most people both inside and outside the system continue to believe that "community" is the most obvious and recognizable characteristic of a Catholic school. Perhaps community is, as it were, part of the spiritual genetic code or DNA of the baptized. Nonetheless most of those involved in Catholic education seem to ever swim against the tide and current of contemporary individualism.

The Need for Community

There exist several reasons why human beings and human institutions, and particularly Christians and their institutions, need a renewed sense of community these days. From both a social perspective and from our theological tradition the Catholic education community has particular reason to be proactive in deepening within all partners a radical sense of community and to challenge the pervasive individualism of today.

The Blishen Report, which examined the Catholic school system in 1989, underlined the fact that the continued existence of Catholic schools depended in no small part upon a communal commitment to the goals and objectives of the system. The various players or partners, according to this report, must agree on what they are about and work together if the system is to have any future.

The report underlined from a sociological perspective the common sense realization that belief can be sustained and transmitted only by groups of people or communities who share faith and values and a common perspective on life and its meaning. Beliefs can be transmitted only within what the sociologists call a "cognitive minority" – a group of likeminded individuals sharing a world view whether the latter is complete or partial.

The words of the Blishen Report in this regard merit repetition: "In the present era of rapid social change, one of the most important conditions for institutional continuity is consensus among members about basic institutional values and objectives …. Since its founding the Church has survived because it has been able to maintain this basic consensus on its objectives. This is particularly evident in the Ontario Catholic school system's struggle for full social and legal legitimacy …. (T)hroughout its struggle for equality of treatment with the Ontario public school system, and despite many setbacks, the Catholic community has continually and consistently proclaimed the essential objective of the Catholic school system. Now that this struggle has been won, the future progress of the system depends, to a large extent, on the degree to which consensus exists on these objectives within the community" (*Catholic Education in the Separate School System of Ontario*, the Blishen Report, 1990, pp. 36-37). In other words from a sociological perspective our future depends on clearly defined communal objectives supported by all the partners.

A second practical reason for community derives from the fact that humankind today is being overwhelmed with the increasing complexities of our world. We now create so much information each day that even the brightest individuals, even the geniuses among us, cannot cope with this information overload. We can now create change faster than we can foresee what such change is going to mean for us. Different systems are breaking down all around us. The continued strife in Iraq and in the Mideast together with ongoing conflicts in several African nations, in Indonesia, the Philippines and elsewhere leave us wondering if world order is even possible. In a world that produces much more food than it needs millions are starving each day. Environmental degradation, the reduced ozone layer and the possibility of nuclear or biological terrorist attacks constitute threats we struggle to contain. In the fields of genetics and biomedicine we are discovering how to tinker with and even create components of the life force, of life itself, all the while recognizing that no individual can possibly know where all of this leads.

Governments, businesses, scientists and industrial concerns ranging from banks to builders of space stations recognize that no individual can deal singlehandedly with the many and complex problems they face. Only people capable of working with a team approach – those who recognize the need of a community of effort to attain the institution, – goals are hired. The practicalities of dealing with the knowledge explosion require if not a community at least a communal effort.

Our Christian tradition has always insisted that our journey in life, of human growth, self-discovery and healing is never to be understood as a solitary undertaking. Our theology or Christian anthropology insists that the "I" or the self grows and is discovered only in relationship with others. Moreover it is in that community of believers which is the Church that the ultimate revelation of the self occurs. It is here that we are redeemed. Karl Rahner and Herbert Vorgrimler's *Theological Dictionary* tells us, "Theology explains and interprets man's (sic) nature as a social being in more detail; man is always the partner whom God has chosen, in such a way that he must realize his personal uniqueness in the community of all men and in its service. God's self communication to all men in Christ has not created a series of private saving histories for atomized individuals, but the one history of the one human race. Yet this history keeps each individual in view for his own sake; but he finds his way to himself – to the person God has in view – only by finding that saving community which God Himself has set up and personally realizing his membership in it" (p. 91).

American scripture scholar Fr. Donald Senior puts it this way: "We are not a gathering of isolated mystics but a people joined by a common life, a common calling and a common destiny with God." God speaks to us seldom in the mountain top experiences of individuals but rather in the nitty-gritty of the community to which we all belong. God's revelation, God's word, God's calling happens not in the splendid isolation of our individual lives but in and through the community to which we all belong. In theological terms it is the community which is the primary *locus revelationis* – the primary place where God reveals Himself to us. We need community to discern in any given moment what God is saying to us. We need community to know who we are and where we are going.

From another perspective there is a visceral realization, a gut instinct, in Catholic life that the living out of our faith is never me alone. For Catholics moments of deep meaning, of birth and baptism, of love and marriage, of the meal of Eucharist, and of death and dying are not moments to be lived alone but with one another. Community may be a reality that is difficult to define, but usually it is easy to recognize.

In her 2004 book *Dark Age Ahead,* the environmentalist and city planner Jane Jacobs echoed the fear of many that a negative aspect of postmodernism is the loss for many of the meta-narrative, the story which provides meaning and direction to human life. Her fear is that we are in the process of forgetting shared values and that this is the way to disaster as history has so often demonstrated. There is legitimate fear as well that Christianity is losing its story, that many who call themselves Christians are functional religious illiterates.

What is often forgotten is that community is necessary to remembering and telling the stories by which people define themselves. Nowhere is this truer than for Christian faith. Christian community is essential to the telling of our story. To know the story of Christian faith and to have it affect our lives requires that we be part of community which has created and tells its story in the scriptures and continues to create and tell this story in the ongoing life of the church. It is the community which gives flesh and blood to the story. It is the community which continues to live the story. In its experience of living the story in different times and places it discovers the language, the symbols, the contemporary idiom to speak again the story and thereby make it comprehensible to succeeding generations. All Catholics, but particularly those who are being initiated into the life of faith, need to be exposed to more than the notions, ideas, words and language of Christianity. If these words and this language are to have transforming effect in their lives, they must also share the experience of people striving and indeed struggling to follow in a secular society the way of life, the journey, as revealed in the gospel story. Such has always been the dynamic of Catholic education.

The Contemporary Challenge – Creating Christian Community

Much has been written in recent years on the distinctive characteristics of a Catholic school. These range from building distinctive curriculum, to pastoral care services, to religious and family life education programs, and so on. The ultimate characteristic, however, that distinguishes a Catholic school is its unique learning environment of Christian community. As mentioned in the preceding chapter the task of continually creating, recreating, fostering and sustaining Christian community as the learning environment of a Catholic school is the ultimate challenge facing Catholic education today. It is a challenge that can be answered successfully only if educators, trustees, parents and parish together acknowledge it as the fundamental and distinctive goal according to which will be measured the success or failure of our schools in the days ahead. In simple terms the effective and successful Catholic school will be the one that creates Catholic community as it primary learning environment.

Ultimately this is a challenge not just for the school system but for the whole Church. Catholic schools alone cannot successfully respond to this challenge. They are, however, uniquely positioned. Like all schools, public and Catholic, the Catholic school often is the single most shared experience of adults. Along with parish, diocese, religious communities and other organizations and groupings, the Catholic school is an institutional expression of the life of the church. And today it is in the school that the present generation of young married couples and their children come in contact with the Catholic Christian community most often. This is where the younger generations of Catholics gather regularly.

More than ever the Catholic school system represents today an incredible human and financial resource of the Catholic Church in Ontario. For some unfortunately it seems to remain a hidden treasure. But with its many well-educated and committed educators, dedicated trustees, supportive parents and involved parish personnel, it is a community poised to provide leadership both in the church and society.

Over almost two centuries the different community partners have taken different leadership initiatives in maintaining and fostering the growth and development of Catholic education. In other times the bishops and priests, the religious and trustees have provided the leadership. In the present era it would seem that the ball is in the court of the educators and those who support them in their task. They would seem uniquely positioned to rise to the challenge of creating

Christian community which will have effect not only in schools but throughout our church in parishes, dioceses and other institutions.

Our history speaks of parents, educators, parish priests, trustees and all of their various institutional structures reflecting not only strengths, virtue and leadership, but also the weaknesses, the failures and the sin of the human condition. None of them is perfect. As earlier mentioned, like the sinful saints who people the pages of our history, those who struggle today to make Catholic education happen are flawed and wounded human beings. They deserve the support of all Catholics as people who often with some reluctance recognize the disruptive call of God as it breaks into their lives asking them to bear a mission of human transformation. Our Christian hope looks to Catholic educators, ordinary people picking up the challenge and achieving the goals of telling our story anew and of creating the learning environment of Christian community in which it must be told.

What Are the Problems/Obstacles?

What then are the contemporary problems facing Catholic educators as they confront the challenge of building the distinctive learning environment of Christian community for Ontario's Catholic school system in the 21st century? One should be disabused immediately of the notion that it is the government that is the primary culprit for the problems we face. The report from the symposium organized by the Institute for Catholic Education late in 2002 indicated significant fracturing of vision and purpose, lack of trust, a need to find common ground within the Catholic education community. More than a few of the participants seemed to lay blame for all that is wrong at the feet of the government. Some at the symposium posed questions such as, "Did we compromise evangelization for funding?" or "Did we compromise our faith agenda/vision for a government mandated vision?" or "Are we suffering the consequences of our acceptance of an empty corporate (business) model for education?" and so on.

There is certainly some legitimacy in these questions.

Finally, however, they represent a too easy escape from confronting the more dangerous internal problems confronting us. In the first chapter it is suggested that we should listen carefully to the wise words of the cartoon character Pogo: "We have seen the enemy and it is us." It bears repeating.

The challenges which most threaten the Catholic school system today don't come from government. Indeed our system, over the last two decades, has made unprecedented advances. With completion of the Catholic system to the end of secondary school and with the same level of funding as our public school counterparts we have achieved goals for which we struggled for decades. Today we have more dollars both relatively and absolutely than we ever had before. This is not to suggest that funding is adequate for all of the tasks now expected of school systems. But it is to say that more serious problems exist within our school community than outside of it, and we should first look to their solution.

The problem more accurately and realistically is defined by significant numbers of the parents and students, and even some educators and trustees, who have only a vague grasp of the Christian story and the tradition which inspired our school system. This is not to question their dedication. But it is to recognize and acknowledge that there is too little clear understanding of and too much warm fuzziness around our heritage of Catholic belief. When much of what we do is distanced from the story and tradition which inspired the Catholic school system; when we seldom celebrate together the meaning of life that is ours in the Eucharist which is at the heart of our faith — when all of this happens there is weakening of the bonds of community. In such circumstances too easily does individualism hold sway for educator, trustee, parent, student and so on. Not surprisingly a widening gulf develops between the different groups and associations of educators, parents, students, trustees, principals and school people in general. Nor is it surprising that there develops great distance between teachers, trustees, other school people and the broad Catholic community.

There is no more egregious example of the breakdown of our community and the distances within it than has been revealed in the last decade when different Catholic education groups have gone to court on opposite sides of various education issues: a fracturing of the community for all to see. One recalls with some pain the scriptural injunction found in the words of Paul in First Corinthians. Writing to this early Christian community he uses language as harsh as one finds in the Christian scriptures. He castigates people for taking their disagreements before the secular courts when he says, "How dare one of your members take up a complaint against another in the law courts of the unjust instead of before the saints." And he continues, "You should be ashamed; is there not really one reliable man among you to settle differences between brothers and so one brother brings a court case against another in front of unbelievers" (6, 6ff.). Today again we might ask if we are incapable of finding mechanisms for resolving disputes within our own community.

Problematic as well is the continuing and too easy acceptance of an adversarial negotiating model for salary and working conditions used by management and employees in the Catholic school system. Over the years it has driven deep wedges within the community. There has been little serious effort on the part of the Catholic teachers' association and the Catholic trustees' association to discover and use other models, even models that have, in varying degrees, proven successful in the business and industrial worlds. Yet still we have those who say that there is no better model than one which in too many cases has created deep and bitter divisions within Catholic school boards.

There are more than enough problems with forming community, but they are not all of somebody else's making. For example, it has been often said that the sense of Christian community in our secondary schools is made difficult or even threatened by the open access provisions of the Education Act. With considerable numbers of students who do not share our faith, who have no sense of Catholicism, who do not participate in liturgy or take religious education courses – with all of this the creation of the learning environment of Christian community is seriously hampered if not rendered impossible. However, the problem is compounded when Catholic boards aggressively advertise their secondary schools to increase grant monies with little apparent concern for how harmful unnecessary numbers of students who do not share our faith will be to creating a sense of Catholic community in a school. The extra dollars that follow these pupils into our schools may turn out to be more harmful than helpful.

In recent years principals have been cut loose from the stability and security of belonging to a teachers' federation. This profoundly alters their relationship with their educational colleagues, the teachers. Less obviously but no less concretely, directives from the Ministry of Education, the Education Quality and Accountability Office and the Ontario College of Teachers have not too subtly changed their job description. Their employers, the boards, seem sometimes lacking in sensitivity to the new situation of their middle management educational leaders. In a time of labour unrest principals can be tempted when conflict arises to deal with teachers not as their educational colleagues but within the strict context of legal and contractual rights and regulations. At a time when Catholic education stands on the fault line of threatened earthquakes both within the church and within the educational world this crucial middle management group can lose any sense of vision as it is buffeted from these and other external forces. They can lose sight of their responsibility to be keepers of the vision in creating Christian community in their schools.

There is something wrong, something significantly wrong. Some have suggested that at the 2002 ICE symposium the participants unfortunately didn't bite the bullet and face the issues squarely. One has to wonder whether as in the Parable of the Boiled Frog we are in a situation where the water has gradually begun to boil all around us yet no one wants to acknowledge the danger.

We are living a moment in the Catholic and Christian community which calls us to acknowledge where we are as a school system and what it is that we wish to be. In the middle of the 19th century as the clouds of the Civil War were darkening in the United States, Abraham Lincoln said to a gathering of the members of his political party, "If we could first know where we are, and whither we are tending, we could then better judge what to do and how to do it" (*Religion Returns to the Public Square*, 2003, pp. 28 and 30).

A New Approach to Creating Catholic Community in Schools

So what to do and how to do it. From the foregoing it should be clear that the Catholic school system would benefit from directing its energies and utilizing its human and financial resources in a manner distinctive to our system. Our leadership, in ways appropriate to our times, is called to create and re-create Christian community as the pervasive and distinctive learning environment of Catholic schools.

In our search for practical ways of accomplishing this goal there exists one contemporary educational recommendation that has particular meaning for Catholic schools – a recommendation largely ignored in our province in the last decade. It is already 12 years since the Royal Commission on Learning in 1995 released its report with four major recommendations for the future of education in Ontario. They were presented as the four engines that should drive educational reform in the years ahead. These engines were teacher professional development, information technology, early childhood education and community education. The last of these is the one that has received the least attention. And yet for Catholic school systems it is surely the one that may be most important for our future. Community education perhaps does not share the glitz of information technology, nor the deserved attention being paid to early childhood education, nor the support of educators for continued professional growth. Perhaps the reason is that there is nothing magic about it. Community education demands the day-to-day grind involved in any community building exercise. It's an expression of education in the trenches.

Yet the approach of community education is essential. The

American sociologist James Coleman has pointed out that schools can succeed only when "first, the school itself, its principal and teachers, has a solid concept of its mission; second, strong families are behind the children; and third, effective communities help to organize the families in support of the schools" (f. Robert N. Bellah et al., *The Good Society*, 1991, p. 176). And the distinguished American educator Thomas Sergiovanni goes further and tells us, "Community building must become the heart of any school improvement effort. Whatever else is involved – improved teaching, developing sensible curriculum, creating new forms of governance, providing more authentic assessment, empowering teachers and parents, increasing professionalism – it must rest on a foundation of community building" (*Building Community in Schools*, 1991, p. xi).

Community education in its broadest sense recognizes that the school lies at the heart of the community; and should be the centre of the community in providing a focal point for delivering a range of services to young people. Community education is about a school or school system acting as the catalyst for encouraging the broad community to come together in identifying and responding to its needs, especially the needs of its children. Community education seeks to redefine or reinvent the relationships between schools, parents and other community groups and create a new synergy within our communities in favour of children. The educational institution provides the focus for the different members and groups within the community to participate in setting the agenda for their identifiable social, educational and cultural needs. In a somewhat narrower sense and without going into all the details community education is about forming alliances between all the many individuals and groups who can assist in the education of children; and it is about providing the necessary education for adults and other institutions so that they can fulfil their responsibilities in the development of our kids.

It could be argued that for many years through the traditional triad of home school and parish, Catholic schools sought to do just this. Few would deny that today, however, the way we involved our Catholic community of parents, parish and educators in the past no longer seems to work. This triad or three-legged stool was based on a different society which was less mobile, with a stay-at-home parent, with well staffed parishes and with teachers who lived within the catchment area of both school and parish. Trying to rejig these relationships and make them work in our contemporary society is a little like tinkering with a Model A Ford to bring it up to speed for our modern expressways. Today even the new kid on the block, which is school councils, doesn't seem to be involving too many parents let alone other community partners in the educational process.

It is at least debatable if the small communities of the past within which the parent-parish-school triad worked are still viable in that shape or form or structure. However, the partnerships are still important. What must be created and re-created are the institutions, the structures that will allow this essential partnership to happen. This is true for all schools. It is of particular importance for Catholic schools.

The concept of community education was advanced by the Royal Commission on Learning as just such a structured manner in keeping with the times, a more structured manner of building community and thereby involving the different partners. For Catholic schools this concept has added value: It holds out the promise of forming the learning environment of Christian community which as we have seen is so vital to any sense of distinctive Catholic education. It holds out the promise of a school system that will hand on to successive generations the truths and values which give meaning to our lives. Creating community is never accidental to the Catholic educational enterprise but at the very heart of what we do. What is being suggested here is that we find the way to do this.

Making Community Education Happen — Some Suggestions

Community of any kind doesn't just happen. And Christian community as the learning environment of the Catholic school doesn't just happen. It requires some vision, some set of expectations, some intentionality, some vision. No matter how one defines the role of principals in schools they are the keepers of the vision; and their expectations, their sense of purpose, their intention or lack of same is in large part responsible for whatever sense of community exists in the school.

Traditionally the principal's role has been defined as educational administrator and curriculum leader. More recently there has been growing realization that catalyst in the creation of community also falls within the definition. Consciously or unconsciously, deliberately or not, principals profoundly affect the kind of community that becomes the school's learning environment. A commitment to community education calls for a new definition of the role of the principal – a new kind of service. However, if principals are to play a pivotal role something must be taken off their plate. If they are to assume new community responsibilities boards must work with these school leaders to assure that this does not become just another task added to their current responsibilities.

For more than 30 years Robert K. Greenleaf's work on "servant leadership" has been widely quoted in business, education, industry and elsewhere as the secular world has grappled with the kinds of leadership needed today. His basic thesis is that the successful leader must conceive his/her role as one of service. It is obviously a concept familiar to those within the Judeo-Christian tradition. Most principals in Catholic schools recognize servant leadership as a hallmark of their role.

What has not received as much attention is Greenleaf's vision of the institution – whatever it may be – of the institution itself as servant. In his essay "The Institution as Servant" Greenleaf argues that not only people such as principals but the institutions they lead could also be servants. In times gone by, he says, caring for persons was largely a person-to-person undertaking in education, in health care and in dealing with other social problems. Now most of this is done in society through institutions. Often they are large and complex, powerful and impersonal, not always competent and sometimes even corrupt. What Greenleaf is saying is that in modern society there is a whole role that we Christians would call caring and healing and reconciling which to a large extent can only be accomplished by institutions and not by individuals. The Catholic school should be such an institution and the approach of community education offers a practical approach.

Practically this calls principals as keepers of the vision to influence and communicate to the communities they serve a vision and a series of expectations for their schools. This vision would be shared with those on their staffs, with parents, with parish representatives. It would reach out to other institutions, groups and associations with the hope of serving them and in turn being served by them.

Most of all teachers, the primary collaborators of the principal, must share the vision. Their role is not to become community social workers but rather to benefit from the community resources made available through community education. But they must share the vision and commitment. Teachers come to the vocation of teaching with enthusiasm and hope and a desire to open the minds of their students to the wonder of learning, of life, of the mystery of the universe and of God. Some maintain this attitude; others unfortunately, even tragically, become jaded under the burden of parental misunderstanding, ministry regulations, board politics, and personal life problems. They close the classroom door and do their own thing in every way. Teaching becomes an individual task in which they wish as little interference as possible. Principals are asked to deepen the awareness of all teachers that much of the learning of their kids happens because of what the school is like and not only because of what happens in their own classroom. Not always an easy task. It is probably a task the principal fulfils not as much in what is said as in the deliberate efforts in a wide variety of ways to continually create an ever deeper sense of community among staff members, and a personal concern for every teacher.

The place of prayer in the daily life of the staff in a Catholic school plays no small part here. If the school day allows quality time for prayer for students it must do the same for educators. Time specifically allotted for staff prayer should be a distinctive feature of a Catholic school. Both individually and communally Catholic educators must have the opportunity to reflect on the calling that is theirs in the midst of all the hubbub which ever threatens to drown out one's sense of vocation in the noise of the day. An old adage of Christian teaching is *contemplata aliis tradere* – we hand over to others what we have prayed on. A commitment to prayer in the school helps give a special face to community education in a Catholic school.

For many educators parent participation in school life is often a difficult if necessary piece of the educational task. Parent interviews and visits to the school, parent-teacher conferences, are sometimes seen as somewhat peripheral to if not interfering with their daily job. This occurs despite the acknowledgement of the indisputable educational research indicating that nothing in the educational process is more important than parental involvement in the education of their kids – and despite the fact that Catholic educational philosophy has always insisted that parents are the primary educators of their children.

Should principals and perhaps their teachers make more forays into the community itself, into the homes of their students? The home and community environments often help educators in understanding and dealing with classroom difficulties, problems and acting out of students. But more than this, such contacts give sure footing to the contention that it is as a community that we are educating our children. Is it possible that Catholic schools might give new meaning and purpose to school councils as an influential vehicle whose primary purpose is to encourage parental participation in their kids' education?

A commitment to community education requires some renegotiation of the relationship between boards and their schools and dioceses and their parishes. In our present circumstances this notion of Catholic community education would seem to look to boards and directors of education with their supervisory officers to pursue this conversation. From the board side there must be insistence on regular meetings with diocesan officials to share and consult regarding the expectations which these different institutions have of one another. In a similar vein should not school boards announce that they will be asking their principals to be in regular contact with parishes with the hope of developing a structural as well as a personal relationship with parishes and their various bodies? Religious education and family life education programs together with pastoral care and chaplaincy services are significant dimensions of the uniqueness of Catholic education. Should not dioceses and parishes, the broad Catholic community, assist in providing the human and financial resources in delivering such programs? Such support is not a new thought. It has been part of the fabric of Catholic education for years.

If community education is to happen Catholic school principals must further develop their relationships not only with parishes but with such organizations as the Catholic Children's Aid Society and its secular counterpart. Regular contact with various health care institutions, homes and hospices that care for the sick and elderly, with correctional services, community and social services and so forth cannot help but benefit the school and the community.

And perhaps most importantly of all in our quest for community, how does the Catholic school as institution reach out to its kids, its parents, its staff members who are hurting? How does it reach out particularly to the dispossessed, the marginalized, those who are found on the edge of the road? A propos of this concern, Jean Vanier advises that "the most precious gift in community is rooted in weakness. It is when we are frail and poor that we need others, that we call them to live, and use all their gifts." A Catholic school community is created when not only a school staff but all those who support the school recognize a common responsibility for the nurture, growth and development of children – for they are always the most vulnerable among us.

For all this to happen educators and trustees must situate themselves within the life of the broad faith community. It is not easy to be a community person today. All involved in Catholic education like many believers today are tempted to go it alone in their quest for God. This too is part of the individualism of our times. The temptation may be particularly strong as our Roman Catholic community is confronted with the sins of the clergy, with the unpopularity of our social justice teaching, and the political incorrectness of opposing things like abortion and euthanasia.

In all of this we might benefit from recalling that from the earliest times followers of Christ have been tempted to separate themselves from the community and find Jesus on their own. Today, as well, there is the temptation (often because of recognized sin within the Church) to forsake the Church and to separate Jesus from the Church. It is true that there can be spirituality without formal religious practice. But to believe in our secular world Catholic educators do need a community, a structure, a place to be before God with other people struggling like themselves.

It may well be that the most important exercise or object of all professional development for both educators and trustees will be discussion concerning the ways of creating community. This should surely be the principal objective of every school principal and staff. They should, as well, be aided in the achievement of that objective by all of the support services for which supervisory officers are responsible.

Thomas Groome, the well-known Catholic educator, points out that our word idiot is derived from the Greek word *idiots*. This Greek word means someone with no sense of others, with no sense of responsibility for others, with no sense of community. We must not be idiots. We must rather assure that for this next decade, for the next century, we and our secular society will continue to recognize Catholic schools and Catholic school systems as places in which education happens in a distinctive learning environment; and that when asked what Catholic schools are about people will still say, "community."

Chapter V

Relatedness, Ambiguity and the Spirituality of the Catholic Educator

Many years ago I went each day into a Grade 1 classroom to witness the introduction of what was then a new catechetical program. One day when I was away a priest friend of mine visited the classroom. Although a devoted and committed priest, his idea of a classroom visit was that unless the kids were climbing the walls when he left the visit was not a success. The next day when I returned the teacher told me that Annette, a wonderfully precocious six-year-old, said to her, "That was a very strange priest who was in here. He should go back to the 'cemetery' for a while because he didn't say anything about God while he was in here."

I have told this story many times because, however else the responsibilities of Catholic educators are defined, the legitimate expectation of professional colleagues, of parents, of the Church community and of the school board is that they say something about God. It is an expectation not unrelated to the seeking for God and the need for some spirituality that arises deep within human consciousness. Today this search for spirituality is a characteristic – perhaps a paradoxical characteristic – of our contemporary secular western world. Everywhere modernity searches for a contemporary spirituality that will say something about God. This seeking is hardly restricted to Catholics or Catholic educators. But these latter are not unaffected by the prevalent disquiet engendered by our cultural environment. They too experience the widespread resistance to a social milieu which seems to so reduce everything to the material and thereby diminish the meaning of life and the human spirit. They too want to say, and to hear, something about God.

Despite, or perhaps because of, the bleakness of our so-called postmodern society countless books, studies and articles these days tell us that large numbers of people in North American society seek a spiritual vision that will provide some meaning, coherence, rootedness and consistency to the journey of life in these often disjointed times. The unparalleled fascination with Pope John Paul II which people throughout the world expressed on the occasion of his death was surely related to the integrity of his spiritual vision – even when people disagreed with him on one or many points. The guru of the sociology of religion in Canada, Reginald Bibby, has pointed out that his surveys in recent years indicate that Canadians – although many often don't go to church or claim any affiliation with organized religion – by and large desire some form of spirituality even if they differ widely on what this means. *Time* magazine a few years ago had a cover story on the number of people who search for some deeper meaning in their lives – people young and old who are involved in different forms of meditation. For some this search for spirituality gets no further than aroma therapy or foot reflexology or a meditative massage. Others embrace aspects of the mysticism of certain eastern religions, or other expressions of what is loosely called New Age religion. The more serious seek, through various forms of prayer and meditation or contemplation, to approach the mystery that they sense transcends their day-to-day interests, concerns and preoccupations. What interests all in their quest is some sense of inner peace and some context that will provide meaning for their lives.

The search and challenge this entails should not surprise us. Most recognize that in this postmodern age we are at a crisis point. We need a new language, a new mental posture that will provide some of the majesty and the mystery, some of the sacredness and holiness, some of the transcendence that secularism seems to have leached out of life. Our hopes for discovering happiness and salvation in science and technology, individual fulfilment and material possessions have betrayed us. Today as the so-called developed world contemplates the phenomenon of creating human life in a test tube, the irony is that many seem to have lost all sense of the ultimate meaning of this life.

Within this climate the educational and social wing of the United Nations commissioned a study asking what the face of education for the 21st century should look like. The Report to UNESCO of the International Commission on Education for the Twenty-first Century is instructive. It underlines that the educational task and process can never be reduced to the pragmatic programming of individuals to fit properly into a utilitarian society. This report, perhaps surprisingly, suggested that education must ever be a spiritual journey. In its words, "There is, therefore, every reason to place renewed emphasis on the moral and cultural dimensions of education, enabling each person to grasp the individuality of other people and to understand the world's erratic progress towards a certain unity; *but this process must begin with self-understanding through an inner voyage whose milestones are knowledge, meditation and the practice of self-criticism*" (emphasis added).

Catholic educators find themselves standing even more uncertainly. They confront not only the cultural earthquake of postmodernism, but also continual educational reform and problems in the Church that further shake the world under their feet.

Not surprisingly those who teach in Catholic schools increasingly find themselves asking whether there is a spirituality that will sustain their lives and shape their striving to create Christian community as the distinctive learning environment in the schools to which they give direction. Most at some time or other and in one forum or the other have reflected on the theology and philosophical underpinnings of our school systems, on how distinctive curriculum must be designed for Catholic schools, on Christian community as the distinctive learning environment of the Catholic school and often – with even more difficulty – on the witness, the ways of acting that our schools request of their educators. But what of the spirituality of the Catholic educator? If all teaching comes ultimately from the heart of the educator, then "Who is the self that teaches?" What overarching personal vision, belief, commitment and conviction can sustain and nourish Catholic educational leaders? These would appear to be questions for our times, questions that call for some exploration – questions regarding what it is we are about in terms of a vision and commitment of life which can provide the inspiration needed to nourish those communities of faith we seek to create in our Catholic schools. There is some urgency in this question. As George Harrison, a member of the Beatles, famously said late in his life: "Everything else can wait, but the search for God cannot wait."

Defining Spirituality

Definitions of spirituality abound. It means much more than knowing how to pray – although that is an essential element. It is about the beliefs, attitudes, convictions and commitments from deep within us which determine our approach to life, to others and finally to God. It is about our heart, about how we see things, how we feel things, and about how these influence the way in which we act and live out our lives. Widely varied spiritualities have abounded throughout the history of humankind. Paul, the apostle, was talking about radically different spiritualities when he wrote in his letter to the little Christian community in Rome, "For those who live according to the flesh, set their minds on things of the flesh, but those who live according to the Spirit, set their minds on things of the Spirit" (Rom. 8:5).

Spirituality is something that is important not only to Roman Catholics or Christians. There are great spiritual traditions, attitudes to life and to others and usually to God in all the great religious traditions – in Judaism, Hinduism, Islam, Buddhism and in native or aboriginal belief systems.

Canadian spiritual writer Fr. Ron Rolheiser, OMI, paraphrases Plato, who says that "we are fired into life with a madness that comes from the gods, and which would have us believe that we can have a great love, perpetuate our own seed and contemplate the divine." According to Rolheiser everyone has a spirituality whether it be life giving or destructive of life. We all have this fire in our bellies. What we do with it is our spirituality. Spirituality he says "… is about being integrated or falling apart, about being community or being lonely, about being in harmony with Mother Earth or being alienated from her" (cf. *The Holy Longing*, pp. 2-12). Our spirituality is about how we deal with the desires that are so much part of our hearts.

More specifically, for the Christian believer, American theologian Richard McBrien states:

> *... to be spiritual means to know, and to live according to the knowledge that there is more to life than meets the eye. To be spiritual means, beyond that, to know and to live according to the knowledge that God is present to us in grace as a principle of the personal, the interpersonal, social and even cosmic transformation. To be open to the spirit is to accept explicitly who we are and who we are called to become, and to direct our lives accordingly in response to God's grace within us.* (*Catholicism*, p. 1019)

Certain approaches to spirituality define and describe what is peculiar to our Christian and Catholic spirituality. Central, of course, to Christian spirituality is that it is profoundly centred in the person of Jesus Christ and in commitment to Him and the meaning His message offers to life. It is rooted in Jesus' revelation to us of a God who is Father, Son and Spirit. "The reason for Christ … is that He might lead us to God," says I Peter 3. So Christian spirituality is founded on our belief in the spirit of God who dwells within us, within our community, and calls us ever closer to the mystery of His self. It is about the message of Jesus that believers understand as the best news they ever heard. It is about knowing and experiencing the person who is Jesus as saviour, friend, brother and as the way to God. Most importantly the message of Christian spirituality, in the words of the English mystic Julian of Norwich, is a message that tells us that "love is the meaning of God."

Although it can be argued that there is really only this one

Catholic Christian spirituality, there are in fact a variety of schools of spirituality, different expressions of this fundamental spirituality within our Roman Catholic tradition. There is Franciscan spirituality and Ignatian or Jesuit spirituality, spirituality that takes its inspiration from St. Francis de Sales, the spirituality of the Carmelites, the Benedictines and so on. There are, as well, Christian spiritualities that spring from the Eastern Catholic Churches, and from Protestant, Anglican and Orthodox traditions. What is very clear, however, in examining the history of Catholic and Christian spirituality in the dictionaries of Christian spirituality is the lack of reference to the life of the average lay person. This is not particularly surprising, for historically, aside from a few identifiable groups (such as the Beghards, the Beguines, or the Brethren of the Common Life) there was little lay inspired or directed spirituality within the church.

To return to our question: what does all of this have to do with the spirituality of the Catholic educator?

Some History Around Our Question

For most of the last 150 years, here in Ontario and in other Catholic school systems as well, the spirituality which has informed and inspired Catholic education and Catholic educators has been a spirituality flowing from the lived experience, the various charisms and spiritual roots of the religious communities who for many years were the backbone and the inspiration for Catholic education. These religious communities provided a priceless gift – a gift which only recently we have come to recognize and appreciate. The spirituality of Catholic education was a result and offshoot of the spiritualities of these various religious communities. Lay teachers were supposed to piggyback, to benefit from the spill-over of the spirituality that developed within and inspired the religious communities whose members taught in Catholic schools.

The question, of course, is what to do when these religious are no longer present in Catholic schools? What must be the new and other spiritual inspiration that must now operate within the Catholic education community? It seems presumptuous to believe that we can continue to live on the spiritual capital of these religious orders of an earlier era.

The educators now responsible for Catholic education in the classroom and the trustees who make policy are lay people. To them Catholic parents entrust their children. No less than the sisters and brothers and priests from earlier times, the Catholic community looks to these lay people to provide some inner direction and inspiration to the lives of these young Catholics. This Catholic educators must accomplish today not inspired by the spiritual traditions of the Jesuits or Sisters of St. Joseph, or the Basilians, or Spiritans, or the Lorettos, but from a spirituality that is peculiar to lay Catholic educators. Just as diocesan or secular priests have gradually come to realize that monastic spirituality does not fit with their vocation, so lay Catholic educators are realizing that the spirituality of religious life does not suit their vocation. It would seem that spirituality for lay Catholic educators must arise from and be connected to their educational experience as married, family, or single people living in the secular, pluralistic and global society of modernity.

In recent years many lay Catholics, and especially Catholic educators, have been grappling as never before with this question of what a lay spirituality looks like. As mentioned earlier, a look at the various dictionaries of spirituality reveals little about this topic. Nor is there much official teaching about a spirituality of family (with the possible exception of John Paul's apostolic exhortation *Familiaris Consortio*), or a spirituality of work (again with the possible exception of his difficult-to-read encyclical *Laborem Exercens*), nor about the spirituality, indeed the sacramentality, of marriage (except for the growing study of his Theology of the Body). And yet these latter happen to constitute the predominant experiences, occupations, commitments and interests of lay people. As well, there is little that speaks directly about the spirituality of the lay Catholic educator.

Already many years ago St. Francis de Sales (1567-1622) was teaching that the path of the spiritual life is not the same for us all. In his classical spiritual work *An Introduction to the Devout Life,* he points out that "devotion (spirituality) must be practised in different ways by the nobleman and the working man, by the servant and by the prince, by the widow, by the unmarried girl and by the married woman ... and must be adapted to the strength, to the occupation and to the duties of each one in particular." Further, he does not hesitate to say that the type of spirituality which is purely contemplative, monastic and religious can certainly not be exercised by all. Rather, he teaches that there are many other types of devotion or spirituality "fit for those who live in the secular state."

Lay Spirituality and Relatedness and Ambiguity

What then might be a contemporary spirituality "fit for those who live in the secular state"? What would be a spirituality assisting lay folk in the search for ever reclaiming their hearts? For weaving together who we are in relation to all that makes up the fabric of our lives?

From a negative perspective it is obvious that a lay spirituality is not one that is inspired and governed by the three vows of poverty, chastity and obedience taken by religious women and men. It might even be asked whether in this day and age the particular spirituality marked by the three vows will best serve as the spiritual basis for Catholic education. Although religious sisters and brothers and priests have moved since the Second Vatican Council to embrace a spirituality that engages the world rather than flees from it, they would be the first to admit that certain aspects of their pre-Vatican II spirituality were anti-world or anti-culture. Vatican II, however, placed Christian life and particularly the life of lay Catholics squarely and necessarily in the midst of this world.

Both our church and our contemporary society are imbued with a new sense of an interrelated global family within which sinful and destructive disparities are daily brought home to us. There is, as well, a cosmic consciousness arising out of the mind-boggling discoveries of the limitless complexity of the smallest observable particles and the seemingly infinite expanses of the universe. These realizations and discoveries pose an ever new challenge to believing people as to how they are to take responsibility for our world as a "divine milieu." Thus the need of a spirituality which both immerses one fully in this world of ours, does not distance us from it, and yet ever pushes us to reach beyond ourselves and our world to the God "from whom all goodness comes."

A first suggestion for such lay spirituality is that it must be rooted in the relatedness which does much to define the human person. For despite the powerful individualistic tendencies that surround and deeply affect western men and women, there lies at the heart of the human person the innate realization that in relatedness we find our selves and our souls – relatedness in the family, in marriage, in work, among friends and colleagues and in society; and relatedness to the creation of which we are the conscious representatives. Such relatedness finds its inspiration, its model and its source in the oft neglected Christian teaching of the mystery of God expressed in a Trinity of persons in loving relationship one with the other.

Within our Christian and Catholic tradition the Trinity is not meant to be some dry and abstract doctrine but a transcendent dynamic of loving persons pushing us ever deeper into the mystery of life, the mystery of creation and the mystery of God. For many Catholics this often seems somewhere beyond their faith experience. Yet such a spirituality of relatedness, for our times and for our schools, for Catholic educators, would seem to be a more pertinent spirituality – one which will best inspire our educational efforts and serve our kids. It is also a spirituality that is often closer to us than we might at first think.

A number of years ago the well-known Catholic writer, Frank Sheed, wrote an article on the Trinity. He began by suggesting that although the mystery of the Trinity was one of our central teachings, it really seemed to make little difference, and have little effect in the lives of most Catholics, in the lives of most Christians. For many years I thought that he was right. Only lately have I come to realize that maybe he was more wrong than right. For although most Catholics do not bother getting into long philosophical and theological discussions about the Trinity, they do try to live its essential meaning in their lives. They do grasp that it is in and through their own personhood and all its relationships that they experience the reality, the presence and the call of God in their lives.

Many Catholics whom I know are not content with the shallow life of short-term and finally meaningless relationships. Many Catholics whom I know recognize intuitively – perhaps as a grace of their baptism – that relationships are what Christianity is all about, and finally relationships are what the Trinity is all about.

Let me try an example: A number of years ago we had a funeral in a parish where I was pastor. It celebrated the all-too-short life of Eddie Lafrance, who was a student at John XXIII school. Eddie grew up in two foster families. The members of these families, together with his schoolmates, teachers, teaching assistants and other staff from John XXIII School, were out in large numbers to commemorate the life and death of Eddie Lafrance.

At John XXIII School he was a fixture. He had been nine years in the Learning Assistance Centre. As the story of his life was told, it soon became clear that Eddie was loved not only by the teachers and assistants, not only by school mates and by the maintenance and support staff. He was loved by all who met him.

There were few dry eyes in the church as those who gathered celebrated the life, death and resurrection of Eddie. He was someone people could love, could relate to. Those who knew him well said that he drew out of everyone associated with him that profound capacity to love, which is God's gift to all of us. From his two foster families, his schoolmates, his teachers and all he knew he seemed to ever draw out and elicit new life and the surprise of joy.

In his passing Eddie again brought life. He gave vital organs to a number of women who would have otherwise died. His lungs went to a middle-aged woman and his kidneys and pancreas to a young woman. And his liver was divided between another woman and a six-month-old girl.

And so it turned out that this multiply handicapped young man, this young man who was confined to a wheel chair and diapers for all his life, this young man whose powers of communication were severely limited, this young man who expressed himself only through body language – it turned out that Eddie Lafrance was a remarkable life-giver. He was a unique person who developed human relationships not only with himself. He also seemed to foster relationships among the various people who knew him. And so he gave life to many both in the 21-year span of his own life and also at the moment of his death. How much poorer life would have been for many if Eddie had not lived.

This story and many of the other important experiences in our lives are about loving relationships. Instinctively we all know that we are at our best, our most human, and our most divine when as persons we are in loving relationships. The reason for this is simple. The reason is that because at these times our true identity, our self, is revealed. Our identity as beings made in the image and likeness of the God who is Trinity – a God who has revealed himself as Father, Son and Holy Spirit in relationship with one another. In these experiences we come to touch the life of the Trinity we have come to know through the human mind and heart of Jesus.

The Trinity tells us that God is not solitary like the gods of mythology or of many pagan religions. He is not capricious or cruel or amoral like the Greek gods. The Trinity says that the mystery of God is the relationship of persons – Father, Son and Spirit – and the basis of that relationship is love. We are made in that image. That is why we are most happy, most fulfilled, and most godly if you will when we too are in loving relationships. When in some way we are Trinity (Rolheiser).

Along with this sense of relatedness another foundation stone for a contemporary lay spirituality would also seem to entail an acceptance in faith and hope of the ambiguity, of the less than perfect, of the uncertainty and mystery of life which is the experience of the daily strivings of most people. When the spiritual life is viewed as journey it will accept the uncertainty in raising kids, in growing in one's love as husband or wife, the uncertainty of the single life which often seems to be outside looking in, the uncertainty in career path as opposed to family concerns, and so on. It seems that a spirituality more accepting of ambiguity can sustain us in these in-between-times as many of the old certainties in Church, culture and civil society no longer seem to provide the guidance and illumination of an earlier age.

To speak of a spirituality that deals with and accepts the ambiguity of life and the less-than-perfect is to speak of a spirituality grounded in the contemporary moment – in all of the search for meaning and relatedness and ambiguity of our post-modern world. Certainly God is given little place in the secular society that surrounds us. Believers struggle today against a secularism that insists that religion, morality and spirituality are purely private affairs having no place in public discourse, in politics and often in discussions about how we educate our children.

We live at a time when, for many, God seems to be absent from their lives or at least present only around the edges. God seems missing not only in contemporary society but in the personal lives of our contemporaries, as well. In the lives of many God seems to have withdrawn, to have disappeared. One has to wonder whether the spiritual emptiness of our era is a contemporary manifestation of the so-called "dark night" or divine absence that seems to characterize the spiritual odysseys of so many of the saints. Or it may be that our spiritual sensibilities have become so calloused that we are no longer awake to His presence. Our senses may have been so dulled by a world vision that is so profoundly materialistic and consumerist that we recognize only dimly the presence and call of God, the need for spirituality within our lives.

Perhaps it is this very darkness and uncertainty that the contemporary believer must dare to embrace. We embrace this ambiguity, however, as Parker Palmer says, "not because we are confused or indecisive but because we understand the inadequacy of our concepts to embrace the vastness of great things" (*The Courage to Teach*, p. 107).

A spirituality rooted in hope and faith in the love of God can accept this less than perfect situation, this world so filled with ambiguity. This spirituality of the pilgrim convinced by the hope that is within us would appear suited to our times. Perhaps it best suits what many believe is a wake-up call from God on the path and journey where many Catholic educators find themselves today. As a Catholic community, as believers, we must surely trust that if the charisms of religious communities which so well served our schools in an earlier day are no longer available to us – we must surely believe that the Spirit has not left us bereft of a guiding spirituality. Such would be a counsel of despair. Rather our hope must have trust in a new lay spirituality that seems to be growing within the Church and surely within those communities which are Catholic schools.

Some Characteristics of Spirituality for the Lay Catholic Educator

If a faith-based acceptance of God discovered through and in all our relationships and a hopeful approach to the ambiguity of life are constitutive dimensions of a lay spirituality, what more specifically might be some characteristics of such spirituality for the Catholic educator? What kind of spirituality – a spirituality that is both relational and accepting of ambiguity – might best serve Catholic educators in this day and age? What would it look like? If spirituality is effectively the way we see things, how we feel about things, our attitude to life, to others and finally to God – if this is what spirituality is, can we discover some distinguishing characteristics of a lay spirituality for Catholic education which will best respond to our current needs, both our personal spiritual needs and those of the Catholic education community? Is there a spiritual approach that recognizes the distinct vocation or calling of the lay Catholic educator – a spirituality arising out of the daily life experiences of the educator, out of the conviction that much of life is about learning, about everyone as teacher and everyone as learner? How will such a spirituality reflect the conviction that good learning and good teaching are more about the search for self and the search for God than anything else?

To be faithful on the one hand to our Christian tradition and on the other hand to be relevant to the world in which we find ourselves, a contemporary spirituality for the Catholic educator might be characterized in several ways. Such a spirituality would be i) incarnational; ii) communally oriented; iii) centred on life; iv) founded on a Christian anthropology and respect for the sacredness of creation; and v) ever cognizant of the fundamental unity between prayer and action.

A Word About Each of These Characteristics

i) An incarnational spirituality is rooted and grows within the daily life experience of the educator. Catholic tradition has always recognized that the face of God is as close as the friend or neighbour who shares my street, my house/apartment, my office or assembly line, my classroom, my bed. It is in the detail of daily life that we believe the glimmer of transcendence peeks out – that every aspect of life betrays the hidden presence of God – that in the starkest and simplest moments grace is to be found. That both in the ecstasy of human sexuality and the pain of death and in everything in between, the word of God finds echo. In the powerful message of the Jesuit poet Gerard Manley Hopkins: "The world is charged with the grandeur of God. It will flame out like shining from shook foil..." And the poet William Blake does not fear to say that "the lust of the goat is the bounty of God."

Catholic educators reflect this incarnational spirituality in the sacredness they recognize in the mystery of each young person, who walks into a classroom. In every kid as attractive or as ragtag or as seemingly obnoxious as they may be we recognize the mystery and promise of life called into existence by a creating and compassionate God – and recognize our call to share in the learning, and the creating and care of this young person. If married with his/her own children, the Catholic educator also acknowledges from experience the wonder of new life to be encouraged and nurtured on the journey of return to this God who is father and mother of all.

In the wonder of something learned, in the pain of children who are hurting, in the fear of parents, in the contrariness of every child, in the hurt of fellow educators — the Catholic educator searches out the constant presence of Jesus, discernible to those who have the eyes to see. The presence of God surrounds us in the untidiness of school politics. In the deliberations and decisions of school boards and teacher unions, in the politics of every school and school council, and even in the seemingly remote decisions of the Ministry of Education a mature spirituality will seek to discern the way of God. More of this later.

ii) This spirituality is, as well, a spirituality of community. Springing from our Catholic heritage, it is based on the conviction that Christian life is not an individual enterprise. Catholic spirituality will ever recognize the place of "personal experience" in our journey to God. This journey, however, is never "a flight of the alone to the Alone." For Catholics, "there is no fully authentic Christian spirituality without the realization of an equal co-presence of our fellow believers with Christ and ourselves, the Church" (Louis Bouyer, *Introduction to Spirituality*, New York, 1961, p. 1029). The face of God reveals itself as we struggle to be community with others. There have always been many faces and expressions of Christian and Catholic spirituality. However, the spirituality of the Catholic educator in keeping with a tradition that goes back to the Fathers of the Church, was expressed by both the great Cardinal John Henry Newman and more recently by such different figures as Dorothy Day and Karl Rahner — the spirituality of the Catholic educator will find itself joined always to and inspired by the teaching or self-understanding of the community of the Church.

In our tradition baptism is the sign, the sacred rite, the sacrament which initiates us into God's life shared with others. All educators know that reading is the gateway to another world. So too, Catholic educators acknowledge that baptism ever pushes us into that world where we become one with the other, become a member of the community of saints, of God's people. Every baptized is given the capacity to handle holy things, to found in marriage a domestic church, to bring to each other the word of God, to learn more about and plunge ever more deeply into the mystery of life of those present with us and those holy people who have gone before us. It is together that we are all called to be saints – saints who live with sin but saints nonetheless.

There appears to be within Catholic life what could be called a spiritual genetic coding, Christian DNA, which demands and enables community. In our educational traditions and practices this is reflected in the unity of purpose and common effort ascribed to family, school and parish in the undertaking which is Catholic education. The spiritual life of the Catholic educator relates always to the community of school and Church no matter how tattered and torn it may be at any given moment.

iii) The distinctive spiritual sensibility and sensitivity of Roman Catholicism has, in recent years particularly, been articulated in terms of what is called the seamless life ethic. This term, coined by the late Cardinal Joseph Bernardin, bespeaks a spirituality that stands always in favour of and protective of life in all its dimensions and manifestations. It calls us to be ever more aware not only of vulnerable kids but of the fate of bag ladies and street kids in downtown Toronto, of tortured prisoners in prisons everywhere, of the starving and malnourished in whatever country, of the defenceless child in the womb and the abused senior in too many residences. It is a spirituality committed to tackling AIDS in Africa, trade barriers and agreements that economically marginalize whole countries – a spirituality that calls us to commit to the sacredness of human life in all its dimensions and to the many questions of social justice and human rights which our late Holy Father so passionately brought time and again to the attention of the world. In other words, it is a spirituality which is prophetically centred on life.

iv) In recent years Catholic understanding has been deepened as we have come to realize that this concern for the sacredness of human life must extend not only to the sacredness of all of life, but to all of creation. We have come to realize that we do indeed stand upon holy ground and must assume responsibility for it. As Vaclav Havel, the poet who became president of the

Czech Republic, has said, "We must divest ourselves of…our habit of seeing ourselves as masters of the universe who can do whatever occurs to us. We must discover a new respect for what transcends us: for the universe, for the earth, for nature, for life, and for reality." This requires a commitment from us and a spiritual vision which stands before the mystery of creation and strives to protect and sustain the environment from which all life springs. We do this because this environment is the creature of God acknowledged by our scriptural teachings as flowing from the "Cosmic Christ" – the Christ whose entrance into our world has radically changed us and it. We as the conscious representatives of all creation stand ever as its defenders.

v) Finally, any spirituality – lay or otherwise – in our Catholic tradition recognizes an essential connection between prayer and action. From New Testament times an essential dimension of Christian life is that prayer without works is dead. Our prayer must issue in our involvement in the concerns we have just discussed. Nor does our spiritual heritage allow for an activism that does not radically derive from a life of prayer. The tradition of our faith is that we can lovingly and effectively grow and stand in favour of life, raise our children, affect and change our world, and care for our planet only out of the richness of our heart, only out of a profound appreciation of life as prayed over (*contemplata aliis tradere*). So we must pray over that which we teach.

Some Consequences

If a lay spirituality for the Catholic educator is one which is incarnational, community inspired, committed to a seamless life ethic, marked by a sense of the sacredness of creation and based on the unity of prayer and action, then some practical applications definitely flow for the Catholic educator.

First of all the incarnate reality for all leaders in Catholic education – and every Christian educator is called to lead – the incarnate world is the world of politics in both its broad and narrow sense. That is the world that affects the Catholic educator's vocation and calling. Many educators decry and shun political involvement as taking them away from their task and vocation. Yet various kinds of politics are very much part of the nitty-gritty world of education. That is where educators do their work, where much of their relatedness is involved, where as leaders in education they live out their journey to God. It follows, therefore, that educational leaders live out their spirituality as Catholic educators by searching out a way of being political that is reflective of Christian life. Rather than describe what this means it might help to look at a Christian role model in this regard. The psychologists are fond of telling us that we all need role models. In an earlier time we called many of them saints.

The way of being a Christian politician is nowhere better defined than in the life of Thomas More. St. Thomas More was the friend and confidante of that mercurial king of England, Henry VIII. More was a wise and worldly man, a man of deep spirituality coupled with a hearty lust for life. And he wasn't a plaster saint in all things if we can believe what some of his family members sometimes said about him. He was as politically astute, however, as one could imagine.

In his introduction to the play, *A Man for All Seasons* — the story of Thomas More — author Robert Bolt has this to say:

> *At any rate, Thomas More as I wrote about him, became for me a man with an adamantine sense of his own self. He knew where he began and left off, what area of himself he could yield to the encroachments of his enemies, and what to the encroachments of those he loved. It was a substantial area in both cases for he had a proper sense of fear and was a busy lover. Since he was a clever man and a great lawyer, he was able to retire from these areas in wonderfully good order, but at length he was asked to retreat from that final area where he located his self. And there, this supple, humorous, unassuming and sophisticated person set like metal, was overtaken by an absolutely primitive rigour, and could no more be budged than a cliff.*

Thomas More was a man of principle who could compromise when necessary, who could plead when it was time to plead and rail when it was time to rail. There is little doubt that in the ambiguity of his political life, he must have wondered often enough about the rightness and goodness of his decisions. But for him and for all who lead in Catholic education it is in this incarnational world that one's faith is lived out. For other models of doing politics as a Christian in more recent years and closer to home one could look with profit at the lives of people like Ed Nelligan, a former director of education with the Toronto Catholic School District Board, and Mary Babcock, a former general secretary of the Ontario English Catholic Teachers' Association.

A consequence of a lay spirituality rooted in community is that the educator will recognize that their professional colleagues, together with parents, students and parish priests, are all brothers and sisters in Christ who not only join with them in common cause, but share a communion of life and meaning. Not only must educators recognize this, but they must go out to meet these people. The challenge of making community education happen for Catholic educators is that they assume some responsibility for making Christian community happen both within and outside the school. Catholic educators must be of the Church and in the Church.

A spirituality rooted in the Christian concept of community will inspire Catholic educators to involve the other educational partners not only because it is good educational practice but because of the conviction that all live life together in a communal bond sharing together baptism into the life of Christ. Such spirituality rejects the notions of "us" and "them," of right versus left, of liberal and conservative, of the parent versus the professional, or the priest versus the principal, of administration and board versus those in schools and classrooms. It is a truly large "C" and small "c" catholic spirituality.

Such community will probably never flow from the school unless it first exists in the staff room. Like any relationship or web of relationships, community doesn't just happen. It gradually grows and develops within the matrix of human contacts that are part of everyday life in a school and outside of school. It is here that principals and other school leaders are called to be pro-active, encouraging interchange among staff members not only in educational matters but on a social level, and yes, on a religious level.

A Catholic educator enlivened by a seamless life ethic will assure that the principles of social justice and concern for the marginalized are reflected not only in curriculum and in classrooms. Commitment to such an ethic will also assure that a concern for justice is reflected in all of the relationships of the school, the staff relationships, the labour relationships and the relationships with students. The dignity of the other professionals, of other workers, and the working conditions of professionals or other school staff persons will be primary concerns of those who administer Catholic schools, of those who provide resource for these schools and for all who teach in these schools.

The spirituality of the Catholic educator then will also reflect a high degree of concern for all students who are on the edge, who are in any way marginalized whether it be by their learning abilities or their economic or social situation. This spiritual vision committed to giving, protecting and sustaining life will lead us always to give a place of privilege to the most disadvantaged of children found within our schools. This surely entails a particular devotion to special education kids – as importunate as their parents may seem at times; and to the families which are most hurting and broken within the catchment area of our different schools. Thus it will be a spirituality that inspires teachers to search out and thereby educate themselves about the family/social milieu from which their students come each day.

Because of our spirituality our kids and the staff within our schools should get some sense, some whiff of the mystery of life and of this universe of ours which we are called not only to admire and exult in but which we are called to nourish and protect. A realization of the transcendent value of all of life and all creation will always be a *leit motif* of Catholic schools. Our students will come to learn that in all of the events that create the fabric of life we stand ever upon "holy ground." The Catholic educator's spirituality will not fear to encounter and lead young people to encounter the mysticism which calls always to the believer.

All of this will happen in relation to the Catholic educator's prayer life. If we are at a time when we struggle individually and as Church to define how this spirituality best expresses itself we still know one thing as certain. It is that just as family relations demand that quality time be given to spouse and to kids, so such time must be given to God. Distinctive Catholic education will flow always from the prayer life of educators as different as their ways of praying may well be. Again what ultimately we will share with colleagues and with our children about life and its meaning is what we possess in our own hearts.

In practical terms this may well mean that in what are at times almost unbearable tensions and indeed suffering in the responsibilities of Catholic educators and their leaders – in the face of Ministry of Education demands that seem not always well advised, of administration that may be perceived as unfeeling or uncaring at times, when confronted with overload in assuring safe schools, necessary discipline, various responsibilities both inside and outside the classroom, and being companion and friend to colleagues – when faced with all of this Catholic educators will ever need an integrated spiritual life to nourish their vision of what Catholic education is all about. To find a way through the political and educational thickets of being an educator today, to shorten the distance between teachers and principals, to deal with overanxious parents, to create Christians community as the distinctive learning environment of the school, to not be off put by the Ministry – to do all this Catholic educators have to give themselves time to stand in the presence of God. For only by searching for a spirituality that will sustain our spirit and reveal our self, only by standing in the presence of God can we hope to stand in our schools and classrooms and fulfil our calling to say something about God.

Chapter VI

New Times, New Leaders in Catholic Education

By far the largest institutional expression of the life of the Catholic Church in the province of Ontario is the Catholic school system. In terms of both human and financial resources it far outstrips all other institutions of the church including parishes, dioceses, and religious communities. With its 36,000 highly educated teachers, it is also the Catholic institution that touches more lives, particularly of young families and their children, than do the wonderful and dedicated but ever greying priests and religious who in large part are responsible for most of the other Catholic institutions in the province.

No one would deny that the school system faces its own problems. As we have seen, the majority of Catholic young people today – even those raised in practising Catholic families and graduates of Catholic schools – have not escaped the profound influence of growing up in a secular culture of practical disbelief. Many may seek a spirituality that will ground them and provide some direction and coherence in their lives.

However, most have minimal commitment in terms of religious belonging, participation in the life of the Church, and are woefully weak in religious literacy. Not surprisingly many of the younger teachers in Catholic schools as part of this generation are not immune from this phenomenon.

Catholic Educational Leadership

It is in this situation those responsible for Catholic education, particularly directors of education, boards of trustees, and all who assist them in the educational task, find themselves today. They face not only a different society but a different Church. It is not too much to say that the form and structure of religious belonging for Catholics has changed significantly. And if this is true then the way we function as Catholics must acknowledge this sea change. If most Catholics touch the life of the Church more at the level of the school than elsewhere, then this must have an effect upon how the various institutions of the Church in Ontario relate one to another and preach the Good News of the gospel. This is the contemporary challenge facing those responsible for the Catholic schools. They have the resources. They must speak to the other institutional expressions of the Church and build the bridges to guide our way into the future. A familiarity with the history of Catholic education reveals that at various times one or other of the partners in Catholic education has had to take the lead. Today it is the schools. Directors of education in particular are in the catbird seat. We live in new times that call for new leaders.

The remarks which follow are an attempt to confront this reality. A thesis is proposed followed by a number of suggestions regarding future development. The thesis that is advanced is not surprising. It may, however, help to provide the groundwork for two needed developments which touch upon the future of both our Church and our Catholic education system in Ontario. These are three main points or pillars. They are points which have been made before.

Three Load Bearing Pillars

The first point recognizes that there are many distinctive features or characteristics of Catholic schools. Curriculum materials specific to Catholic schools have been developed in all subjects and disciplines. Continued attention has been paid to our unique pastoral care services, religious and family life education programs. There is distinctiveness to be found even in the particularity in school construction, management/labour relations and so on. Ultimately, however, the Catholic school is distinguishable from public or secular schools because there is a fundamental difference in the intentional learning environment which Catholic schools seek to create. That unique learning environment which is both the genius and the hallmark of a Catholic school is Christian community – a place and space where the echoes and presence of God are everywhere. The intention of the Catholic school is that in this learning environment all education takes place. All efforts in curriculum development, the professional growth of educators, the building and financing and administration of Catholic education are intended to support the creation of this learning environment of Christian community. It is meant to be a community which in many ways is ever questioning and challenging the dominant and pervasive community and culture which so affects (and educates) the lives of young people and us all.

Christian community is the ethos, the atmosphere, the environment, the milieu that is intended at once to inform, inspire and transcend all the different subjects and disciplines taught in the school. Interestingly "community" was clearly identified by Catholic and non-Catholic, by young and old, and across all parts of the province, as the first recognized characteristic of Catholic schools in a study using focus group research and commissioned by the Ontario Catholic School Trustees' Association in 1996. Community is the glory of Catholic education – recognized by all. To some extent this may seem to be wishful thinking because such community is always marked by the imperfection which is part of the life of every Christian. But despite the acknowledged imperfection community in Catholic schools stands at a clear remove from the disquieting legacy of isolated individuals lacking any sense of rootedness which community provides. Modernity or postmodernity or secularism has left many in our western world almost unconsciously seeking something better than the experience of alienation, fragmentation and cultural desolation which follows upon the isolation of individuals.

In an earlier time in our Canadian and Ontario society Christian family, parish and school were socially, psychologically and geographically close to one another. In such times it was perhaps in unconscious or implicit fashion that we recognized the task of continually creating, recreating, fostering and sustaining Christian community as the primary task of the Catholic educator. In contemporary Ontario society, however, the social, psychological and geographical distances between the partners are much greater. As well, in our times none of us is untouched by the above-mentioned pervasive individualism of our secular postmodern world. To create Christian community as the Catholic school's distinctive learning environment can no longer be taken for granted. This would seem to be the most pressing challenge which we face. As proposed in Chapter Four, it would not seem excessive to say that all partners in our Catholic school system in consensual fashion must make of it the fundamental and distinctive goal according to which will be measured the success or failure of our schools in the days ahead. In the language of effectiveness and accountability: the effective Catholic school will be the one that creates Catholic community as it primary learning environment; and for this it should be held accountable.

The second point or pillar of this thesis is that every Catholic Christian community is dependent upon and takes its life, its spirit and its inspiration from Eucharist, which is the source and summit of the Christian life. Without Eucharist we cannot have Catholic Christian community. It is by Eucharist that we define ourselves. It is in and through Eucharist that we gather as believing people to celebrate who we are. In this regard it helps to remember that in the days of the early persecutions of the Church the Roman authorities had a hard and fast criterion for identifying and for condemning a Christian. The criterion of the Roman courts was that one was a Christian not primarily in terms of dogmatic beliefs, nor in terms of moral codes. These were important but the ultimate criterion, the one that provided sufficient evidence for conviction, was participation in the liturgy of the early church, participation in the Eucharist.

In an increasingly unbelieving world Eucharist is the occasion for us to stand together before the mystery of life's journey.

It is where we lean upon one another and accept the solidarity of human weakness and woundedness. Eucharist is where we respect the value and dignity of each other. And perhaps most importantly today Eucharist is of its very nature "structured dissent from the pervading culture of narcissism." It is a protest against the self-absorption that so easily overtakes us. In Eucharist we genuflect before something greater and more wonderful than ourselves. In the words of the English Redemptorist Denis McBride, the Eucharist remains always "something that is beyond us yet is mysteriously part of ourselves." Unfortunately we live now a moment in the life and history of the Church in western society where the large majority of baptized Catholics have only a passing and superficial attachment to and relationship with the Eucharist. These are not bad people but good people who are in large part religiously illiterate and casually unaffiliated. They are people who may believe but who choose not to belong.

Many of us are so completely and often unconsciously immersed in the culture of our times that we are unaware of its effect upon how we think, how we feel, what preferences we have and what we deem to be important including the kind of importance we attach to the education of our children. All of us in our western world are fed every day a secular postmodern message of relativism, temporary commitment and the need for individuals to get ahead of the rest of the pack. We also face each day a new secular fundamentalism – not religious fundamentalism but secular fundamentalism which would allow none – but its ideology to shape life in the public forum. Somehow or other there has been leached out of life much of the sense of the sacred, of the mystery of life and of the wonder of the common humanity which finally should give us our definition and self-understanding. So in the lives of many baptized Catholics Eucharist fails to resonate with their experience even though they send their kids to Catholic schools.

The third and final point is that it is within these circumstances, in this climate of little Eucharistic practice, in this climate of the secular, of individualism, of half belief, non-belief and misbelief we are challenged to continually create, foster, develop and maintain the learning environment of Christian community within the Catholic school system. Confronted with this challenge we face significant odds. To face these odds with any chance of success it would not seem much of a stretch to suggest that we move with some sense of urgency to foster a sense of a lay spirituality, and a Eucharistic spirituality, for Catholic educators. For more than two decades now our schools have been the privilege and responsibility of lay people – teachers, trustees, principals, supervisory officers and directors of education almost all of whom are lay people. Most of the people in leadership positions through a variety of courses have had the opportunity to familiarize themselves with good thinking on the philosophy or the theology of education. However, as underlined in our examination of a contemporary spirituality of Catholic education, this is not enough. There remains a pressing need to discover a Christian and Catholic spirituality for the Catholic lay educator.

A search for spirituality already described in Chapter Five accompanies the above-mentioned search for God. It is everywhere evident in today's society. Signs of this search surround us. People are enrolling in everything from courses on meditation techniques, to the practice of Yoga, to various New Age spiritual prescriptions to foot reflexology and aroma therapy. Unfortunately many seek this spirituality as a kind of relaxation therapy. They want spirituality without the commitment, the sacrifice and the discipline which must accompany it.

A Christian spirituality rejects none of these methods or techniques out of hand. It does insist however that any Christian spirituality does involve commitment and discipline. More specifically for the lay Catholic educator, much of life is about learning, about everyone as learner and everyone as teacher, a world that at least implicitly recognizes that good learning and good teaching are more about the search for self and the search for God than anything else. The world of the Catholic educator is also a world of good kids and difficult kids, of the joy of discovery, of harried parents, of misunderstandings, of unions and professional colleagues, and of all the political processes necessary to achieve one's educational goals and aspirations. It is from these worlds and within these worlds that the spirituality of Catholic lay educators is to be discovered.

To recap: Christian community is the distinctive learning environment of the Catholic school. Such communities find their inspiration and meaning in Eucharist. To continually create, foster and develop such communities Catholic educators must have a sustaining spirituality.

Two Needed Developments

To move such an agenda forward in the current moment of Catholic education in Ontario there are two needed developments, two possibilities in the making, full of both promise and problem. Like most possibilities found in significant moments they admit of some ambiguity. They are challenging developments that can lead us to deepen and strengthen the Catholic educational project and the life of the Church or, if ignored, they can weaken our efforts to find our way into the future.

The first possibility relates directly to the unique position occupied today by the directors of education in Catholic schools in Ontario. They are the leaders, the chief educators, of what are currently the most significant, the most visible and probably the most influential institutional expressions of the life of the Church. In this responsibility they are accompanied in various ways by all who provide Catholic education. This Church of ours has always expressed its reality throughout the centuries in a wide variety of institutional ways. We have dioceses, and parishes, religious communities, social welfare agencies, health care institutions, and so on. At various times and in different places these institutions have preached the gospel and exercised considerable influence not only upon their particular members and concerns but upon the whole Church.

Effectively today we live a situation where young Catholics, young families – the future of our country and our Church – learn from lay educators who under the guidance of the director of education create the environment of the Catholic school. This is the reality. It is not the result of a planned process or a strategic plan. But it is the reality. This is the Church to which they belong.

Without analysing why this is so it should at least be noted in passing that Catholic school systems are demonstrably different from many other institutional expressions of Church life. They are governed by democratically elected members of the Christian community. They subject themselves to clear and public if imperfect requirements of accountability and transparency. Our school systems are related to and are inserted at least partially in the broader secular education processes of the province. They strive through regular and intentional programs for continued professional growth in all disciplines including courses dealing with the traditions of our faith. These same schools and school systems are committed to the rights of individuals, recognize gender equality, and are much inspired in their direction by women who form the majority of the educators. For these and many other reasons they have relevance on many levels – a relevance that appeals to their constituents surely but to many other believing people as well. Part of this appeal lies in the fact that these schools strive ever to be Christian communities which give consistency, coherence and an ultimate sense of purpose in a society and at a time in which any sense of vision seems lacking. One cannot ignore the fact, however, that in this Church institution the Eucharist is not ordinarily celebrated and this is part of the ambiguity that must be faced in this situation.

Effectively this means that directors of these systems of Catholic schools and their collaborators are crucial to the future direction not only of these school communities but of the Church. It is possible that only a few consciously recognized or reflected on this aspect of their responsibilities when seeking to be a director or an educator in any capacity. Indeed it will not be the first occasion where circumstances have changed an educator's job description. Many might not really have wanted to get into this role. Like getting married and most other vocations, only afterwards do all aspects and responsibilities dawn on most husbands and wives, priests and religious. But directors – and many Catholic educators – are today significant

Church leaders. Probably like the Hebrew prophets Jeremiah and Isaiah more than a few would have some difficulty in accepting this role, this ministry. Indeed like these two prophets they might have to be dragged kicking and screaming into acceptance of this ministry. When he became aware of what Yahweh called him to do Isaiah's first words were, "What a wretched state I am in! I am lost for I am a man of unclean lips, and I live among people of unclean lips..." (Isaiah 6:5). Jeremiah when first recognizing his call responds, "Ah, Lord Yahweh; look, I do not know how to speak; I am a child" (Jer. 1:6). Towards the end of John's gospel Jesus says to Peter, the one he has chosen to lead in a special way, "I tell you most solemnly, when you were young you put on your own belt and walked where you liked; but when you grow old you will stretch out your hands, and somebody else will put a belt around you and take you where you would rather not go" (John 21:18).

To believe in the mystery of God at work in our personal journey is to believe that most often we are where we find ourselves to be in life because of the pull of God. Catholic directors of education and their collaborators are not found in the positions they occupy only because they were hired by their board, or because they were approved by the Minister of Education, or because they have the requisite degrees, experience and education. They are where they are because they are called by God.

If this thesis is correct then the greatest challenge for directors and their collaborators is bringing the people who make up the school community to pull together in creating Christian community. Certainly as much if not more than bishops, priests and religious in the contemporary Church, Catholic educators today are called to prophetic action, to take the lead in making this happen. Today's secularized men and women seldom hear the gospel or encounter Christian community in church because they are seldom there. Nor is it likely that they will pay attention to the message of the gospel even if it is preached and shouted more often and more loudly in any other forum or medium. However, they and their children may experience the great Good News of Jesus; they may back into the gospel, if you will, if they encounter in a school a Christian community which with all its imperfections and sins is recognizable as struggling to live the values of the gospel – if they encounter a place where they experience those values of freedom and truth which many fear our society has given up on.

The most significant resources, both human and financial, of the Catholic community are found today within the school system. Billions of dollars are expended each year for Catholic education. Well educated and dedicated professionals staff the schools. Trustees, the directors, and their close collaborators – supervisory officers, principals and other leaders, and ultimately and especially the classroom teacher – touch the lives of more of the baptized than do many if not most priests and religious. There has to be explicit recognition of this new world, and of the new roles within it. In some way in the Church in Ontario the way we function as church and our structure as Church has to more explicitly and intentionally acknowledge this reality.

Within the life of the Catholic Church in Ontario directors and their collaborators are in the catbird seat. As in no other time in our history they have the opportunity to reach out to the other institutions of the Church, to the other partners and invite them into newly formed organic relationships. Signs of this taking place are already seen in areas in the province where boards have taken leadership in bringing together parishes and dioceses, and other Catholic agencies and joining in common cause to assure new life in the community.

There are an increasing number of "best practices" to which one can turn – best practices of reconstituting those relationships which have always made Catholic schools unique communities of faith and unique learning environments. Included in these best practices are diocesan organizations that seek to bring together all Catholic service organizations, community centres which again bring together all the supports and services necessary for a community to work, and education initiatives that reach out to the adult population in a wide variety of ways. Moving in these kinds of directions are institutions like the

Council of Catholic Service Organizations in Hamilton and the new Catholic Education Centre in Waterloo, Adult Learning initiatives in Ottawa and the long-time Thunder Bay Diocesan Trustees Organization. All these best practices recognize that if Christian community as the primary learning environment of a Catholic school is to be maintained, there will be required a communal effort. Finally, what is required is the effort not by one board, not by individual boards, not just by the school system but by all parts of the Church – and that it is the school system that is best positioned to make this happen.

It cannot be pretended that all of this happens easily. Within the Church as outside, institutional pathologies remain which fear both the requisite change and the surrender of autonomy which such changes require. School boards and educators at all levels, diocesan and parish officials have allowed great distances to develop between them in recent years. Too many are into the "blame game." There exists, as well, in all of this a constitutive ambiguity. As already mentioned, by definition schools are not the ordinary place where Eucharist is celebrated. The role of leadership which falls to the school must work to assure the necessary and organic relationship with the parish, which is the ordinary gathering place of the worshipping community.

But to assure the continuance of the Catholic school system such initiatives must happen as we Christians, Catholics and all believing people are confronted with increasingly formidable odds. The growing ideology of secular fundamentalism, already mentioned, works "religiously" to create a social fabric in which the religious voice is banned from the political world, the scientific world, the economic world, and the educational world. Our courts grow increasingly wary of the concept of communal rights and seem almost bewitched by the primacy of individual rights. I think most recognize in more reflective moments that constitutional guarantees alone are not going to assure the continuing existence of the Catholic school system as the only publicly funded religious system in our increasingly pluralistic society. It can be argued, however, that if we do maintain the uniqueness of our Christian communities, many of our fellow citizens will want to share our kind of education. Rather than abolish Catholic schools they will prefer to have similar schools where believing community is the primary learning environment.

So the first challenging development or possibility highlights the prophetic leadership roles that directors and other Catholic educators are called to. And might I add that it reflects a notion and understanding of Church as being first of all and above all God's people finding their way in the different moments and situations of our collective life.

The second needed development or point is a corollary. As effective and dedicated as directors may be they cannot wage this battle alone either individually or aside from the rest of the Church. But they occupy a unique position to profoundly affect the future of Ontario's Catholic schools and of the Church in Ontario. It seems highly unlikely, however, that this can happen without some very thoughtful and dedicated human resources to assist them. Directors, indeed the Catholic system, need as never before such resources and these resources are not obvious. We need a resource bank of people schooled in the tradition and heritage of Catholic education, in the best of our philosophical, theological and spiritual thought on Catholic education.

Much of my reflection on this point was occasioned during a couple of days working as a resource person with the people from the Catholic boards in Ontario who belong to the newly established Catholic Association of Religious and Family Life Educators of Ontario (CARFLEO). The members of CARFLEO are, as their title indicates, the religious and family life education people of our Catholic school boards. At this event a young man asked me — I thought as diplomatically as possible — who were the people who would be providing resources for future meetings of such groups as CARFLEO. As gently as possible he was saying, "You're an old man, and thanks for coming. But what about the days ahead?" And he was right. We don't have much bench strength.

There are a limited number of such human resources available. Some exist among the membership of the directors and supervisory officers and principals and teachers associations. But as far as I can see – for whatever reason – directors don't often invite other directors or other resource personnel into their boards. Nonetheless the situation remains that we need expert and knowledgeable people who will provide "think tank" expertise to directors. We need research and development people assisting directors in the strategic planning for the days ahead. We need people who will identify the "best practices" of the community working together, families, parishes, boards, schools and dioceses. I remember a friend of mine who worked as the religious education consultant for a board telling me that some day when the director walked into her office and asked what she was doing she was going to reply, "I'm thinking." We need people who are going to do some thinking so directors and their boards can more clearly identify where they must go and how to get there.

We need research and development people who will keep us ever conscious of how much secularism threatens to flatten the Catholic imagination, to flatten the ways and the words we use to think about and imagine God. These "think people" will assist schools to be in the forefront in the ongoing search for a new language of faith. We are slowly fashioning this new language in the Church and schools may well be where the wordsmiths can best practise their trade. Already schools recognize, perhaps faintly, the power of some new words to communicate and to transform – words of contemplative stillness; of new expressions of community where gradually faith is fostered; of practical service to the wounded where faith is modelled (cf. Michael Paul Gallagher's *Clashing Symbols: An Introduction to Faith and Culture*, 2003). Many students and their parents today distrust the possibility of truth and experience in their lives much unfreedom. Perhaps only faintly our schools can be communities of truth and experiences of freedom, and so speak words of truth and freedom so many wish to hear.

Directors and their collaborators are accustomed to utilizing expert opinion. When boards are challenged with serious problems: improving numeracy and literacy; when they launch school construction projects; when they tackle the intricacies of school finance, they avail themselves of the assistance of people expert in these fields. As mentioned at the beginning, two of the most serious problems we face are maintaining a sense of Christian community and assisting our professional educators to develop the lay spirituality that will sustain these communities. Boards need expert help in these areas and it will not be provided save by a leadership initiative from every level of the Catholic school system.

Most boards individually probably cannot afford this resource – although some might say they cannot afford not to have it. But surely, collectively, some plan could be put in place to assure that such resource is available to the Catholic education community in Ontario. Perhaps it would be through utilizing the existing facilities of the Institute for Catholic Education (ICE) in new ways. Perhaps it means more funding so that ICE can realize more of the research objectives contained in its original mandate. Maybe it could be a collective undertaking of ECCODE, the association of Ontario's Catholic directors of education. Maybe it means more co-ordination of programs in Christian leadership offered at the University of St. Michael's College, St. Jerome's University and currently being instituted at York University. The point is that despite these initiatives we appear to lack the human resources to plan effectively, currently and for the future. As well, many of the marvellous young teachers in the system are often woefully weak in their grasp of the story that binds us together, what the system is all about, where it came from; and possess a very hazy vision of where it should go.

What I am suggesting is the need for a co-ordinated effort on the part of directors of education so that boards take the lead in mobilizing the above-mentioned resources to address this deficit. Because few boards, if any, could do this alone it would seem that it would best be done together.

The oft quoted principle of subsidiarity cuts both ways. It means not only that what can be done at the local level should be done at that level. It also means that when we cannot do something at a lower level and in singular fashion then we should band together in doing it collectively.

To create Christian community inspired by the Eucharist as the unique learning environment of the Catholic school requires on the part of all partners a vision, and a spirituality which will enliven and inspire this undertaking. It is in such communities of faith that all the partners will continue the mystery and wonder of Catholic education which is time and again to allow the echoes of the mystery of God to be heard in the hearts of children and all whom the Catholic school touches.

Chapter VII

Catholic Education and the Search for Truth

Most Catholic educators would agree with the argument made throughout these pages: the ultimate and defining characteristic distinguishing the Catholic school from public or secular schools is a fundamental, indeed, radical difference in the intentional learning environment which Catholic schools seek to create. That unique learning environment which is both the genius and the hallmark of a Catholic school is, as we have discussed, Christian community. In recent years Catholic educators have sought to define and describe for both Catholic and non-Catholic alike a number of defining characteristics of a Catholic school community.

As described earlier these characteristics range from building distinctive curriculum in all subjects and disciplines, to pastoral care services, to religious and family life education programs, to school construction, management/labour relations and so on. But it is the distinctive learning environment which creates our uniqueness. And in this intentionally created educational culture, as we have seen in the third chapter, a primary educational objective must be to assist students to discover and discern the truth – the truth of all of life, the truth of myself, the truth of this marvellous universe of ours and the truth of God. We seek this truth with the conviction that its deepest meaning is found in light of the message and meaning of Jesus Christ. As the gospel of John tells us: "I was born for this, I came into the world for this: to bear witness to the truth; and all who are on the side of truth listen to my voice" (John 18:37).

Increasingly our Catholic theology and self-understanding derive inspiration from a world view or cosmology that underlines the relatedness in the meaning of human life, the wonder of the universe and the mystery of a compassionate God, the transcending source and sustaining power of all creation. Within this world view the community of the Catholic school dedicates itself to the search for the truth of the human person, the truth of the wonder of all creation and the truth of the mystery of its Creator.

The search for this truth is not easy. The accomplishment of this goal is rendered difficult today as never before. It is compromised by the dominant pluralist and often secular culture of the western world which often dilutes and relativizes the meaning of truth if not altogether denying the possibility of its attainment. For many what is true and what is good is whatever the majority in a democratic society decide. The result, as pointed out by Pope John Paul II, is that "this has given rise to different forms of agnosticism and relativism which have led philosophical research to lose its way in the shifting sands of widespread scepticism." Recent times, he said, "have seen the rise to prominence of various doctrines which tend to devalue even the truths which had been judged certain. A legitimate plurality of positions has yielded to an undifferentiated pluralism, based upon the assumption that all positions are equally valid, which is one of today's most widespread symptoms of the lack of confidence in truth" (*Fides et Ratio*, para. 5).

From a less philosophical perspective this giving up on or trivializing of truth is seen all around us. In the media the relativizing and the manipulation of truth is so prevalent that one hardly notices it anymore. We seem strangely content to live in an era of what we recognize as disinformation. We watch and listen to TV and the web, read our newspapers and listen to radio with increasing scepticism. We have been subjected to too much "spin." We observe with jaundiced eye as too often the media fasten on the sensational and disregard the reality of the down-to-earth ordinariness out of which most of the fabric of life is spun. We grow increasingly disenchanted with TV and radio reports which highlight cameras and microphones thrust in the face of the grieving or distraught. News as entertainment enjoys stories which not only report conflict but feed on it to the detriment of honest efforts to resolve the conflict.

In the political world the truth of promises has become the fodder for stand-up comedians. South of the border then President Bill Clinton told us categorically, "I did not have sex with that woman." His successor justifies war in Iraq with reports of non-existent weapons of mass destruction and non-existent alliances with al-Qaeda. Here in Canada we have dealt for many months with the lies and dishonesty associated with the sponsorship scandal.

In the business world a person's word is no longer accepted as their bond. The words Enron, WorldCom and Nortel speak of lies that have ruined the lives, destroyed the careers and stolen the pensions of untold thousands. It is little wonder that the American novelist Saul Bellow sadly writes, "… public virtue is a kind of ghost town into which anyone can move and declare himself sheriff" (quoted by Bloom, p. 85).

The world of institutional religion does not come away unscathed. There has been in our Church the obvious failure of accountability if not outright deception in the scandal of sexual abuse. Not so readily recognizable but even more disconcerting is the flight by many believing Christians to a kind of religious fundamentalism that gives the lie to serious theological and scriptural investigation, and would so leave believers with a faith that abandons reason by the roadside.

In the educational world discussions between teachers, parents, trustees and other partners too often betray a quest for power and monetary advantage under the guise of better education for children. An egregious example has been the attempts for decades of some trustee and teacher groups who have sought the demise of the Catholic education system under the pretence that thereby better education would be offered to all Ontario's children. In like fashion salary negotiations in all the publicly funded systems are conducted supposedly with the good of students in mind when in reality they are contests of strength and power where what matters is winning and not the truth.

In the world of sports, athletes, in everything from the Olympics to professional games such as baseball, track, and football to the Grand Prix of cycling, are regularly compromised by doping scandals. When confronted with test results the reaction of most athletes is to blatantly deny any involvement in the use of illegal drugs. They "fess up" only when caught with evidence that is incontrovertible.

In the halls of academe – in the university world – traditionally the bastion of truth in civilized societies, the firestorm of deconstructionism still blows so strongly that many intellectuals, particularly in fields such as literary criticism and history, seem often wary of lifting their heads above the trenches. The "hermeneutic of suspicion," very legitimate and helpful in itself, has intimidated many scholars in their quest for truth. Fortunately the more recent sobering second look of people such as those associated with the Euston Manifesto recognizes and respects historical truth and seeks to question scholarship which rejects out of hand, as historically conditioned, research which doesn't meet the criteria of the politically correct. This same group of self-described left-leaning scholars and commentators calls out for a needed "political honesty and straightforwardness."

Only "science" – and specifically so-called "hard" science – seems to escape the prism of an examination of the motivations of the writer or researcher. And this mindset has filtered down in society to the point that my eight-year-old nephew a few years ago could hold up one of his text books and proclaim proudly to me, "Everything in here is true – it's science."

Universities further compromise their reputations as searchers for truth as they continue to offer scholarships to the athletically talented who are fine athletes but hardly students. As well, university students buying essays on line and plagiarizing viewed as wrong only if they get caught.

One barometre of the pervasiveness of untruth is reflected in the still popular sit-com *Seinfeld* – almost a cultural icon in the entertainment world. An article by Canadian veteran journalist Robert Fulford on this program points out that the most obvious attribute of all four characters is dishonesty. "They're all liars!" a correspondent wrote to him. They constantly lie, to strangers and to each other, without a second thought. "He's right," Fulford says. And he continues, "But what does it say that neither I nor anyone I've read on *Seinfeld* noticed? I think it says that routine lying is more widely accepted than we would like to imagine" (*Globe and Mail*, May 21, 1997).

All of this is part of the culture of our time. It is a culture which often seems either not to believe in or to have any commitment to the possibility of truth. It affects not only the lack of trust that we have in one another as individuals. It also brings into question whether societies, particularly democratic societies which we so cherish, can survive as our levels of trust diminish. Sisela Bok in her book *Lying: Moral Choice in Public and Private Life* limns this disquieting scenario:

> *As lies spread – by imitation, or in retaliation, or to forestall suspected deception – trust is damaged. Yet trust is a social good to be protected just as much as the air we breathe or the water we drink. When it is damaged, the community as a whole suffers; and when it is destroyed, societies falter and collapse.* (pp. 26-27)

In his first New Year's message Pope Benedict XVI said: *We need but think of the events of the past century, when aberrant ideological and political systems wilfully twisted the truth and brought about the exploitation and murder of an appalling number of men and women, wiping out entire families and communities. After experiences like these, how can we fail to be seriously concerned about lies in our own time, lies which are the framework for menacing scenarios of death in many parts of the world. Any authentic search for peace must begin with the realization that the problem of truth and untruth is the concern of every man and woman; it is decisive for the peaceful future of our planet.* (New Year's message: "In Truth, Peace," para. 5)

It is in this atmosphere that the Catholic school and the

Catholic educator is challenged not to give up on truth – to remain convicted that the truth and only the truth will set us on the course to human freedom. Indeed the document *The Catholic School* tells us that the purpose of all education from a Catholic perspective is to "help (the student) spell out the meaning of his/her experiences and their truths" (para. 27). The community of the Catholic school finally is the environment which creates the space for a teacher to lead students to practice the search for truth.

To declare that the search for truth is a defining characteristic of the Catholic school is to raise the bar in an educational world where many have given up on the possibility of truth. Allan Bloom argues in his analysis of American education, *The Closing of the American Mind,* that "almost every student entering the university believes, or says he believes, that truth is relative," and that relativism is the "only virtue which all primary education for 50 years has dedicated itself to inculcating" (pp. 25-26). Whether or not one agrees completely with Bloom, it is difficult to deny that there is a strong whiff of reality in what he says. Truth in our time is questioned, denied or ignored in almost every aspect of our contemporary society including the world of education. Like a dangerous and odourless gas, the disregard for truth affects and infects all aspects of our lives.

Education and Truth

The Catholic educator does not have to be a doomsayer, a latter day Cassandra, to grow fearful of what effect such a climate and culture has on the education of young people and of all citizens. Teachers more than most acknowledge that even more than the family or the school it is this culture so doubtful of truth that is the principal educator of us and our children. These are the waters we swim in and the air we breathe on a daily basis. For this reason there is needed more than ever before countercultures like the Catholic school to act as a reality check which commits itself to truth and to the search for truth. The debate may rage forever as to whether one can be good or have truth without God. The faith conviction of our religion remains that with God we can have truth and be good.

Part of our Catholic tradition is that faith is not a mindless exercise; that Catholicism is a religion with a brain, and that truth exists and is attainable. As the Dominican Timothy Radcliffe so aptly puts it, "… what is strikingly different about Christianity is not that Christians are better than other people and so less inclined to tell lies. What is distinctive is twofold: in a skeptical world we believe that we can attain the truth through thinking. Second, our faith gives us a rather different understanding of what it means to be truthful." He then quotes fellow Dominican scholar Yves Congar: "I love truth as I love a person" (*What is the Point of Being a Christian?*, 2005, pp. 113-14).

Ingrained in our religious tradition and heritage as Christians is that we are ever called to be searchers and witnesses of the truth. The biblical notion of truth is that it is in the truth that we meet with God. And the fullness of this truth is encountered in the person of Jesus Christ, the Word, the utterance, and the Son of God. The First Letter to the Corinthians calls us to be "… the unleavened bread of sincerity and truth" (5:8). The Letter to the Ephesians exhorts the believer to be a person "speaking the truth in love." And the First Letter to Timothy insists that Christians are to be a people "which upholds the truth and keeps it safe." Jesus in the gospel of John tells us that it is the truth that will set us free (8:32); and that "he is the way, the truth, and the life" (14:6). The final and ultimate conviction of the believer is that God himself, "the Spirit is truth" (I John 5:6).

If the Catholic education system is to justify its existence not only to Catholics but to the broad society, if it is to make a recognizable contribution to public life and discourse – then it will always be in our efforts, albeit tattered at times, to be an intentional community of those who seek to speak, reflect and be in service to the truth.

If they are recognizable for their commitment to the search for truth, Catholic educators will provide a service not only to the kids in their classrooms but to our contemporary society. If they regard themselves, their students and their colleagues as truth seekers they will respond to a hunger of this postmodern world. It is not only in fiction like Douglas Coupland's *Life after God* that one hears echoes of this hunger. Consistently surveys such as those done by Canada's own Reginald Bibby and the European Values Study reveal dissatisfaction with a one-dimensional, material and relativized world. As well, the day may be passing us by where postmodernism celebrated the provisional, discontinuity, fragmentation, subjectivity and incoherence. Increasingly from different perspectives and for different reasons, there is a mounting search for the transcendent and the spiritual. There seems to be in contemporary society a growing awareness that truth matters and that it relates to God. Today it is asked if the absence of truth relates to the absence of God. Is there is a connection between the eclipse of God and the crisis of truth in western society? The question is raised, as well, whether there can be any truth in love without some divine reference.

In our human understanding we seem to be growing beyond a reductionism that would reduce everything to genes and molecules and social and biological conditioning and electrical impulses. We don't believe that that's all there is. We grow weary of the jingoism of the molecular biologist who describes us as "no more than numbers in a cosmic lottery without a paymaster." Perhaps this latter day world of postmodernism is witnessing people grown weary of skepticism. Having deconstructed everything from history to literature to the behavioural sciences we find ourselves like the Irish playwright Samuel Beckett's workman who hears his colleague call out, "Don't come down the ladder. I've taken it away." Without a ladder of meaning we dangle between absurdity, boredom, suffering, death and the absence of God.

The Catholic school system and its educators stand at a critical juncture. From the riches of our tradition we have a contribution to offer in how education in truth should be done. To approach this task Catholic educators are reminded, however, of the old spiritual adage that "humility is truth." So it is not with proud assertions and thundering proclamations but with the humility of the searcher that Catholic education speaks of and seeks truth. We are increasingly abetted in this task by the scientific world which has shed some of its own hubris and acknowledged the element of mystery in its quest for knowledge. Thus cosmologists and other scientists who seek some kind of unified world view examine such previously unlikely theories as the so-called "string theory" — a theory that speaks of a reality that admits of many more dimensions than the usual space-time continuum recognizes. There is the mystery of so-called dark matter, the gravitational force that holds galaxies together and which represents 25 per cent of the universe. There is the little known force of dark energy, the anti-gravitational force that pushes the universe to ever expand. It constitutes 70 per cent of the universe. Astrophysicists tell us that, though these cannot be seen, their effects are recognizable.

Together with the scientific world believers are increasingly convinced that there is more to truth than what the hard sciences can tell us - that being able to measure things is not the only criterion of truth.

New Truths for our Times

Despite the individualism and disjointedness that so mark western society, both our church and our contemporary society are imbued with a new sense of relatedness and a new realization of how all in life, all in this universe of ours, is interrelated. Especially do we realize how profoundly the lives of all of us are interrelated. The latest earthquake in Indonesia, the ongoing effects of Hurricane Katrina, the floods in Bangladesh, the climate of global terror which seems to strike ever closer to home in these last days — all speak of interconnectedness for good or for ill. The new global society forces us in the developed world to realize that if we care millions will live — and that if we do not care then people elsewhere die.

There is, as well, a new cosmic consciousness, a sense of relatedness, arising out of the mind-boggling scientific discoveries that reveal both the limitless complexity of the smallest observable particles and the seemingly infinite expanses of the universe. More importantly our science has taught us how these infinitesimally small particles and waves and massive cosmic systems relate to each other. We now know that we share a common origin with the smallest neutrino and with the vast and great reaches of our universe. We have all come from the gases and the fires of the Big Bang. We are made of the same stuff. We are related because we and everything else in our universe comes from the same cosmic dust. We are part of a "divine milieu" and must accept responsibility for all peoples and creatures of which it is made. We must accept responsibility because we are related to it all. It is a world that is ever expanding beyond itself. And this world seems ever to push us to reach beyond ourselves and our world to the God "from whom all goodness comes."

The theologian Richard Cote, who worked with the Canadian Conference of Bishops for a number of years, has pointed out that we live today a moment when the most fruitful scientific models seek to reunite much of what has been divided since the Enlightenment.

> *Unlike Enlightenment models, according to which science alone seeks truth and delivers realistic insight, and unlike the perspectives of deconstructive postmodern theorists which ascribe only a functional value to a word like "truth " – a perspective being true only in the sense that it is capable of illuminating a partial aspect of reality – constructive postmodern models regard the reality of truth (and the truth of reality) in much more holistic terms, that is, in terms of the interconnectedness and interplay of all beings, human and non-human.* (*Revisioning Mission: The Catholic Church and Culture in Postmodern America,* p. 144)

In other words, if we are tuned into our western world we hear echoes of a brand new search to discover and to make happen all that would bring us together, with our brothers and sisters, with our environment and with our universe.

This is the cultural surround in which Roman Catholic schools exist. We seem called today to consciously and intentionally put our minds to the first question asked by Jesus in John's gospel: "What are you looking for?" This becomes the foremost question Catholic educators today put to themselves and to their students, "What are you looking for." The answer of course is truth. For it is truth that will reveal to us the meaning of ourselves, our neighbour, our God, and all of his creation.

In his encyclical *Fides et Ratio,* late Pope John Paul II described the fundamental search for truth which concerns people of all religious and philosophical traditions:

> *... a cursory glance at ancient history shows clearly how in different parts of the world, with their different cultures, there arise at the same time the fundamental questions which pervade human life: Who am I? Where have I come from and where am I going? Why is there evil? What is there after this life? These are the questions which we find in the sacred writings of Israel, as also in the Veda and the Avesta (the scriptures and prayer book of Zoroastrianism respectively); we find them in the writings of Confucius and Lao-Tze, and in the preaching of Tirthankara (in Jainism, a religion of India) and Buddha; they appear in the poetry of Homer and in the tragedies of Euripides and Sophocles, as they do in the philosophical writings of Plato and Aristotle. They are questions which have their common source in the quest for meaning which has always compelled the human heart. In fact, the answer given to these questions decides the direction which people seek to give to their lives.* (para. 1)

John Paul II described the Church as being in a special way at the service of this search for truth. "The Church serves humanity with the *diakonia* – the service – of truth. We are partners in humanity's shared struggle to arrive at truth" (ibid., para. 2). No institution of the Church is more clearly called to this role of service than the Catholic school. The wonderful and challenging vocation of Catholic teachers in this vision is to be a servant of the truth.

As described in our introductory remarks, there is little doubt that the search for truth has been grievously wounded in our times; and yet the quest for the truth of ourselves, our universe, and our destiny ever haunts that desire for personal integrity which resists the reductionism that would belittle the human spirit. In the words of Sisela Bok: "The role that one assigns to truthfulness will always remain central in considering what kind of person one wants to be – how one wishes to treat not only other people, but oneself" (Bok, p. xix).

This is the privileged task of all educators, but for Catholic educators who believe that truth resides ultimately in the mystery of the God of the universe it is a task that takes on special meaning. How then is the Catholic educator to accomplish this task? What follows are a few suggestions.

Educating Students to Search for and Discern the Truth

As educators approach the world of their students – and their own world – they must recognize that we live today in our society and our church a moment of profound transition. If young people have not changed – and most would agree that they have not – the world in which they live has changed radically. On the one hand theirs is a world of untold promise and possibility of literally reaching for the stars. The world of communication technology with its computers and internet and Blackberries and iPods has put the world's knowledge at their fingertips. On the other hand the kids who come daily to our classrooms see, hear, touch, feel and experience few clear universal values which support and hold the world together. Theirs is a discontinuous and fragmented world. They do not readily experience and comprehend life as holistic and integrated, and they wonder about it. At an educational symposium in March of 1987, Mario Cuomo, who was then the governor of the state of New York, told of a conversation he held with a young teenager in the school yard of a New York City school. Governor Cuomo had spoken to a couple of hundred ninth and tenth-graders about the danger and madness of using crack cocaine. He spoke about the beauty of life, the opportunities in their future, and the threat to all their hopes and dreams that crack posed. In other words he described an integrating vision of life.

After he finished, he asked them if all of this made any sense. He describes their reaction in this way: "Most of them nodded. One didn't. A boy, maybe 15, with a chipped front tooth, looked at me with his head half-cocked to the side, his face impassive but his scepticism showing through quite clearly. 'Didn't you agree with me?' I asked. 'That your life is too precious to give away to drugs?' 'I'm not sure,' he answered. 'The stuff you said sounded good, but I don't really know. I'm not sure what my life is really for, why we're here. I really don't understand it.'"

The reaction of this young teenager in New York city unfortunately no longer has the power to surprise us. It is the reaction of a young person who has learned well – who has learned all too well the lessons our society has been teaching for too many years. The lesson of our postmodern and deconstructed world too often is the lesson of scepticism, of doubt and hesitancy to commit despite the marvels and miracles of our scientific and technological advances.

When he visited Canada in 1984 and met with Catholic teachers in Newfoundland, Pope John Paul II said to them:

> *Young people today are buffeted in every direction by loud and competing claims upon their attention and allegiance. From around the world, they hear daily messages of conflict and hostility, of greed and injustice, of poverty and despair. Amidst this social turmoil, young people are eager to find solid and enduring values which can give meaning and purpose to their lives. They are searching for a firm place – a high ground – on which to stand.*

Our kids and ourselves grapple with and live in this world of modernity which has morphed into postmodernity. It is a world in which the synthesis of self, neighbour, community, creation and the universe, and God fell apart. It was this situation that Vatican II sought to address. Throughout our Judeo-Christian history it is clear that our image and understanding of the mystery of God has ever deepened. Vatican II sought to present an image of God for our time. It spoke of a faith and a God characterized not so much by obedience and conformity as by freedom, a search for the truth of life and a spirituality which plunges one into the mystery of this God. This Council's image of God reflected the gratuitous goodness of the God of Israel, the God who called for love and mercy rather than sacrifice. A practical example of this wiser appreciation of God is told by the late British Cardinal Basil Hume in his book *Basil in*

Blunderland:

> *He had been told by some grown-up that he must not take things from the larder without permission. . . . Why not take one? Nobody would know it. It just seemed common sense. Nobody would see him. Was that true? Nobody? One person would. That was God. He sees everything you do, and then punishes you for the wrongdoing, so I was told.*
>
> *It took me many years to recover from that story. Deep in my subconscious was the idea of God as somebody who was always watching us just to se if we were doing anything wrong. He was an authority figure, like a teacher or a policeman or even a bishop.*
>
> *Now many years later, I have an idea that God would have said to the small boy, Take two.*

Those who teach in Catholic schools in whatever subject or discipline, those Catholic educators committed to encouraging their students in the search for truth, recognize how the lives of their students are daily affected. They face the reality of students who like their peers in other schools have their imaginations and values shaped more by the web, Britney Spears, U2, rap music, reality TV and video games than by the gospel. It is not that these influences are necessarily bad in themselves. It is that alone they can leave young people with imaginations that are stunted, memories with vast holes in them and emotions that lack the grit of reality. In the Canadian Giles Blunt's 2005 murder mystery *Black Fly Season*, the character "Red" sustains a traumatic head injury. As she is examined by the doctors and questioned by the police it becomes clear that she has not only lost her memory. She has also forgotten how to feel, to care, to fear, etc. In today's cultural surround one asks what the dangers are of today's young people forgetting much of what it is to be human.

Without rejecting what is good in contemporary culture and youth culture, educators seem especially called today to lead students to reflect on and recognize how this culture affects their thinking, their imagining and their emotions. At the same time they will seek to bring to the surface, to awaken the natural questions which are part of the growth of young people. It should be underlined that this is not a process of evangelizing them or catechizing them and certainly not a process of indoctrination. Rather its purpose is to assist students in what in an earlier time was the educational process of analysing and of comparing and contrasting the realities which they daily encounter. In this case it involves analysing, comparing and contrasting the multiple values which so captivate youth – especially those values of teen and pop culture reflected in the entertainment and media worlds. And it involves relating these values to the deep hungers that young people discover within themselves. Simply put, educators will be leading young people to discern the reality and the meaning of what happens daily in their lives. This obviously is not the responsibility only of the religion teacher but of all teachers in a Catholic school. Let me make clear that all of this search for truth which gives us our identity is not about fleeing from our secular culture but constructively engaging it in a critical way. It's about Christian faith as a truth detector.

Only when the kids recognize the truth of what happens in their lives; and only when they acknowledge a thirst for some coherence and meaning – only then can gospel values get through the many filters which society creates in their minds. Obviously for younger students this may mean no more than intentionally exposing them to what is beautiful, what is great and good in the wonder of creation and the mystery of the human spirit. As they grow more mature it means that older students are invited as much to reflection and the search for wisdom as to the accumulation of information.

It is when young people can clearly recognize the values of their culture and the stirrings of their hearts that the values of the gospel will strike a responsive chord and be heard as having meaning in their lives. Only then can they recognize how the gospel can speak to and shape their culture; and how in turn their culture can further break open the deep meaning of the gospel.

This is what *The Catholic School* from the Congregation for Catholic Education means when it suggests that all educators in every school are called "...to formulate the concept of school as a place of integral formation by means of a systematic and critical assimilation of culture" (para. 26). Further, for Catholic schools it says that such is accomplished by "... a synthesis of culture and faith, and a synthesis of faith and life" (para. 37).

Today Catholic education will especially be about teaching kids how to assess and evaluate, how to discern the significance of all the experiences that make up their daily life. So it will not just be about teaching them the catechism or the gospel or Bible stories or Church teaching. Indeed before evangelizing and catechizing, i.e., before proclaiming and explaining the gospel, the Catholic educator will teach a process of discernment – of how to discern what is good and great, what is beautiful and true and just. It is about awakening in students (and ourselves) ever deepening desire to examine all that they experience in their culture and constantly ask what all this means for their own life.

Catholic education from this perspective means examining all that makes up the fabric of our contemporary culture. It means acknowledging the scientific wonders, the literature and music and cultural and social richness of our times. And it means not limiting the educational task to acknowledging this richness and these wonders but involves the attempt to plumb their deepest significance as they point beyond themselves. Catholic education is not about rejecting contemporary culture, science and technology but in discerning their deepest meanings and directions from the perspective of the human spirit. It is about bringing the insight of God's word to every dimension of the fabric of life; and it is about allowing the gospel in turn to be enriched as the mystery of the universe further reveals itself to the questing human intellect. This is the truth which Catholic schools are ever in search of.

There has always been much talk in the educational world about the "hidden curriculum." The hidden curriculum consists of all of the implicit assumptions of those who write programs and texts and subject outlines for courses as diverse as economics, politics, history, literature, chemistry and even mathematics. Even more important is the recognition in curriculum of unannounced and implicit values such as competitiveness, submissiveness, docility and deference to the detriment of imagination, creativity, independence and so on. Usually this curriculum agenda is as much the agenda of the society as it is of the school. As such it can too easily buy into that secular fundamentalism which would leach all of the wonder and grandeur and marvel out of the human journey.

What Catholic schools are asked to do is to lead students to examine all the agendas that impinge upon their lives particularly those hidden agendas that the dominant culture proposes – and to relate these agendas to the truth of the students own lives and to the truth of the gospel.

In its 1995 report, Ontario's Royal Commission on Learning spoke of the need for developing in young people what they called different "literacies." The commission spoke of "literacies" such as communication skills, numeracy and problem solving, group learning and interpersonal skills and values, scientific literacy and computer literacy. As well, this report spoke of education which would lead kids to "think, create, analyse, reason, debate, synthesize, understand, communicate, learn and keep learning" (p. 9 of *A Short Version of Living and Learning*). What is being suggested here is that in Catholic schools there be a clearly defined objective of developing a "literacy" of discernment of the truth – an objective of developing in students the mental and psychic and imaginative apparatus to search for truth.

Two Corollaries

1. Associated with this search for truth in Catholic education is the acknowledgement of the longing for spirituality which is at the heart of most of our contemporaries - especially the young. The Australian poet James McCauley writes of the young as religiously disinherited: "Who do not think or dream, deny or doubt/But simply do not know what it's all about." Yet there remains that sense of unease, of incompleteness resulting in a spiritual questing. This search for spirituality can be many things, but for the sincere in heart it is a search that acknowledges the mystery of life and the need to enter more deeply into that mystery. This spiritual hunger of our times betrays a quest for the mystical which affects more rather than less of the people we meet each day.

In the book *Girlfriend in a Coma*, author Douglas Coupland wonders, "There must be all these people everywhere on Earth, so desperate for the smallest sign that there is something finer or larger or more miraculous about ourselves than we had supposed. How can I give them a spark?" (quoted by Michael Paul Gallagher in *Clashing Symbols*). This surely is the question of every Catholic teacher: "How can I give them a spark?"

Not surprisingly this search has occasioned a turning of our theology to a new attention to a loving God discoverable in the lives of all. Our theology speaks of a spirituality which embraces mysticism. The Latin American theologian Leonardo Boff writes that "Mysticism is not the privilege of the fortunate few. It is rather a dimension of human life to which all of us have access when we become conscious of a deep level of the self, when we try to study the other side of things, when we become aware of the inward richness of the other, and when we confront the grandeur, complexity and harmony of the universe. All of us, at a certain level, are mystics" (*Ecology and Liberation: A New Paradigm*, 1995, pp. 147-48). And the great German theologian, Karl Rahner, many years ago did not hesitate to say that "the Christian of the future will be a mystic or he (sic) will not exist at all."

Young people share in what has become a deep longing in our times – a longing to see beyond the superficial, to touch the mystery of this universe of ours in all that is human and non-human. It is one of the "signs of our times." It is a truth that is universally sought and Catholic schools must be in the forefront of responding to this quest and curiosity that ultimately is about wanting the immediacy of God in our lives (cf. Richard Cote, *Revisioning Mission*, pp. 152ff.).

With a certain justification some will point out that the

Church recently has not distinguished itself in providing an adequate response to this contemporary spiritual longing. They say that its institutional and dogmatic concerns have got in the way. The result is that people have looked elsewhere. Be that as it may Catholic schools as the institutional expression of the church closest to young people must give priority to the awakening and nurturing of this spiritual hunger among our students.

2. Related to all of this is the natural idealism of youth which questions always the injustices and violations of human dignity. They have a natural affinity for the social justice teaching of the Church. They instinctively recognize the untruth of the economic, social and political realities which leave so many of the world's people by the side of the road. Theirs is an innate sense of justice relatively untouched by compromise. The phenomenon of world wide communications, especially the web and TV, has made them citizens of the world. Their perspective on social justice is a global one. And they realize that efforts to achieve social justice demand a kind of partnering, a solidarity and common effort that eschews the individualism that surrounds them – and that speaks ever of the God of our tradition and heritage.

The lack of equity in the distribution of the world's resources, the denial of fundamental human rights such as food and health care to billions of people stands as an unfulfilled challenge to the gospel of Jesus Christ. Our generation and the ones preceding it have left this challenge unfulfilled. This is an opening through which the word of the God of our ancestors seeks to be heard. This is fertile soil indeed for the Catholic educator. To help students comprehend the social teaching of the Church is to put them into contact with a truth that has the promise of becoming one of the inspiring voices in the great debates of our era.

For Catholic educators accomplishing this will mean resisting some of the educational agenda that others would impose. It may be helpful to examine with students and colleagues the implicit educational objectives in curriculum materials from the

Ministry of Education. Or to ask how significantly the educational objectives of the business community such as those proposed by the Conference Board of Canada affect the way we do education. Even many parents sending their children to Catholic schools give priority to educational goals that have more to do with financial success in life than to a successful Christian life. (See for example the Blishen Report.)

Students can be led by teachers in Catholic schools to sniff out how the school itself and its programs are subtly hijacked by the values of the dominant culture. The Christian ideals of school mission statements and of other Church institutions can be examined to discover how faithful we are to the social truths we endorse. The truth of Catholic social teaching is hard-edged. It will not accept what Michael Warren calls a "Jesus reduction program" that nicely fits the "aspirations of middle-class culture" (*Communications and Cultural Analysis*, p. 13).

Lighting the Fire

In many ways all believers and believing Christians and Catholic educators find themselves in a foreign land these days. We speak a language – a language of faith – that many do not understand. Missionaries preaching in foreign cultures have always had to discover a process of inculturation. They have had to learn and discover a new language – but not just the words and grammar. They have to learn and discover the metaphors, the imagination, the symbols of that culture as the keys that unlock the story of the gospel, the story of faith, to their hearers. In like fashion in the present moment the symbols, the metaphors, the language and the culture of today (particularly of the youth culture) have to be learned by those who would teach. This approach to Catholic teaching is much more than simply tuning into the songs young people sing, the TV they watch and the films they go to. Knowing these has value but there are deeper myths or archetypes in our culture – myths and archetypes which yield deeper meaning and open up the meaning of the gospel.

As new missionaries in a foreign land, Catholic schools can with their students seek a language that critically embraces the metaphors of our postmodern culture and of the youth culture and so reveal anew the rich truths of our faith. They can awaken a sense and apparatus of discernment, and a commitment to the truth of justice, and an imagination that will provide the language that brings together our faith and our culture.

Catholic teachers are called to give emphasis to the need for community in this age of individualism, to the need for generosity of spirit in an era of conspicuous consumption, to a spirit of sacrifice to confront the seduction of hedonism. Perhaps more than ever today, however, within its unique learning environment of Christian community a Catholic education system must ever give primacy to the search for truth.

If you are familiar with the legends that speak of the ministry of St. Patrick in Ireland you will know that the pagan druids were the reigning religious authorities. Each year the druids came together as was their custom to celebrate the rebirth of the sun after it had died in the winter. On Patrick's first year as a missionary this druid feast coincided with Easter. As was their practice the druid religious leaders lit a fire to celebrate this occasion. All the other fires in the area were to be extinguished, with the idea that they'd all be relit from this one fire.

In the darkness of the night and in the darkness of then pagan Ireland, however, Patrick, in view of all the people lit his own bonfire. On the Hill of Slane he lit his fire to announce and celebrate the truth of the risen Christ. This was tantamount to a declaration of war against the druids and their King Laoghaire. Patrick and his followers were soon arrested and put on trial in Tara before the king. It was said that the druids told the king, "If that fire is not quenched today it will burn for ever, and it will overcome all the fires of our religion."

The king, however, not only pardoned them, but he also allowed them the right to preach the gospel throughout the whole land. The light of their fire, according to author Thomas Cahill in his *How the Irish Saved Civilization*, provided "a living alternative" to a pagan people who lived in "quaking fear" of monsters everywhere and the threat of sudden death. Within only a few generations, the Irish were busy sending out missionaries, and preserving the literature of classical civilization. The druids were right about St. Patrick's fire. God used it to ignite a blaze in the hearts of the Irish people. And all of it happened because one man wasn't about to hide his light under a bushel.

Like Patrick's fire on the mountain, there is a light of truth that can shine forth from Catholic schools and so speak to all in our society. This truth must not be hidden under a bushel. In this way our schools will be recognized both for their distinctiveness and for an ever more important contribution to the life of our province and our country whose people so much want to know the truth of life.

Suggested Reading

Bibby, Reginald, *Restless Churches*, Novalis, 2004.

Bok, Sissela, *Lying: Moral Choice in Public and Private Life*, Vintage Books, 1999.

Canadian Catholic School Trustees Association, *Build Bethlehem Everywhere: A Statement on Catholic Education*, 2006.

Cannato, Judy, *Radical Amazement*, Sorin Books, 2006.

Vatican Congregation for Catholic Education, *The Catholic School*, 1977.
The Religious Dimension of Education in a Catholic School, 1988.

Cote, Richard G., *Re-Visioning Mission: The Catholic Church and Culture in Postmodern America*, Paulist Press, 1996.

Gallagher, Michael Paul, *Dive Deeper: The Human Poetry of Faith*, Darton, Longman & Todd, 2002.
Clashing Symbols: An Introduction to Faith And Culture, Darton, Longman & Todd, 2003.

Groome, Thomas, *Educating for Life: A Spiritual Vision for Every Teacher and Parent*, Thomas More, 1998.
What Makes Us Catholic: Eight Gifts for Life, Harper, 2002.

Institute for Catholic Education, *Catholic Education in the Separate School System of Ontario (The Blishen Report)*, 1990.
Ontario Catholic School Graduate Expectations, 1997.

Leddy, Mary Jo, *Radical Gratitude*, Orbis Books, 2002.

Mulligan, James T., *Catholic Education: Ensuring a Future*, Novalis, 2005.

Ontario Catholic School Trustees Association, *Witnesses to Faith*, 1997.
Involving Other Parents: The Primary Focus of a Catholic School Council, 1999.

Ontario Conference of Catholic Bishops, *This Moment of Promise*, 1989.
Fulfilling the Promise: The Challenge of Leadership, 1993.

Palmer, Parker J., *A Hidden Wholeness: The Journey Toward an Undivided Life*, Jossey-Bass, 2004
The Courage to Teach, Jossey-Bass, 1998.

Radcliffe, Timothy, *What is the Point of Being a Christian?*, Burns & Oates, 2005.

Report of the Royal Commission on Learning (Ontario), *For the Love of Learning*, 1994.

Rolheiser, Ronald, *The Holy Longing: The Search for a Christian Spirituality*, Doubleday, 1999.
The Shattered Lantern: Rediscovering a Felt Presence of God, Crossroad, 2001.
Secularity and the Gospel, Crossroad, 2006.

Sacks, Jonathan, *The Dignity of Difference: How to Avoid the Clash of Civilizations*, Continuum, 2002.